THE WIND IN THE WILLOWS

A Fragmented Arcadia

TWAYNE'S MASTERWORK STUDIES: CHILDREN'S AND YOUNG ADULT LITERATURE

Robert Lecker, General Editor

THE WIND
IN THE WILLOWS

A Fragmented Arcadia

Peter Hunt

TWAYNE PUBLISHERS • NEW YORK
Maxwell Macmillan Canada • Toronto
Maxwell Macmillan International • New York Oxford Singapore Sydney

Twayne's Masterwork Studies No. 141

The Wind in the Willows: A Fragmented Arcadia
Peter Hunt

Twayne Publishers   Maxwell Macmillan Canada, Inc.
Macmillan Publishing Company   1200 Eglinton Avenue East
866 Third Avenue   Suite 200
New York, New York 10022   Don Mills, Ontario M3C 3N1

Library of Congress Cataloging-in-Publication Data

Hunt, Peter, 1945–
  The wind in the willows : a Fragmented Arcadia / Peter Hunt.
    p. cm.—(Twayne's masterwork studies; no. 141. Children's and young adult literature)
  Includes bibliographical references and index.
  ISBN 0-8057-8816-6 (cloth).—ISBN 0-8057-8817-4 (pbk.)
  1. Grahame, Kenneth. 1859–1932. Wind in the willows.
  2. Children's stories, English—History and criticism. 3. Pastoral fiction, English—History and criticism. 4. Animals in literature.
  I. Title. II. Series: Twayne's masterwork studies; no. 141.
  III. Series: Twayne's masterwork studies. Children's and young adult literature.
  PR4726.W515H86   1994
  823'.8—dc20   94-15213
                                                              CIP

The paper used in this publication meets the minimum requirements of American National Standard for Information Sciences—Permanence of Paper for Printed Library Materials. ANSI Z3948–1984. ∞ ™

10 9 8 7 6 5 4 3 2 1 (hc)

10 9 8 7 6 5 4 3 2 1 (pb)

Printed in the United States of America

For Chip and Ann Sullivan
who know all about good friendship, and fantasy, and
food, and the riverbank life of North Carolina and
Gloucestershire

Contents

Note on the References and Acknowledgments

The edition of *The Wind in the Willows* used in this book is the Charles Scribner's Sons, published by Macmillan, New York, 1989. It contains an article by Ernest H. Shepard, "Illustrating 'The Wind in the Willows.'"

Kenneth Grahame *(1859-1932).*
Reproduced by permission of the Bodleian Library, Oxford, England.

Chronology:
Kenneth Grahame's Life and Works

1859	Kenneth Grahame is born on 8 March at Lasswade, Scotland, the third child and second son of James Cunningham Grahame and Elizabeth (Bessie) Grahame.
1860	The Grahame family moves to the Inverary area of Argyllshire in the west of Scotland.
1864	Bessie Grahame dies of scarlet fever in April, shortly after giving birth to a fourth child, Roland. The children are sent to live with their maternal grandmother at "The Mount," Cookham Dene, in Berkshire, England, thirty miles west of London on the River Thames.
1866	Cunningham Grahame moves to Fernhill Cottage, Cranbourne, and summons the children back to Scotland, where they stay for nearly a year.
1867	Cunningham Grahame's health and mental state decline; he goes to live abroad and has no further contact with his children.
1868	Grahame is sent to St. Edward's School in Oxford, where he begins to display his rebellious streak.
1875	Grahame's elder brother, Willie, dies. Grahame leaves school.
1876	Grahame is unable to attend Oxford University, ostensibly for financial reasons. Instead, he takes a job as a clerk in his Uncle John's London office, Grahame, Currie and Spens. In London, he meets F. J. Furnivall, who later goes on to found the Early English Text Society.
1879	On 1 January, Grahame enters the Bank of England as a "gentleman-clerk."

1880	Grahame becomes Honorary secretary of the New Shakespere [sic] Society, a position he will keep until 1891.
1882	An attempt is made to assassinate Queen Victoria.
1883	Karl Marx dies.
1884	Grahame begins voluntary work with the poor, which he continues through the 1880s. He visits Cornwall in the west of England, where he learns deep-sea fishing.
1885	The Pall Mall Riots take place in London, and widespread looting takes places in Picadilly, evidence for conservatives such as Grahame of dangerous changes in society.
1886	Grahame visits Italy, which begins a lifelong fascination with southern Europe.
1887	Cunningham Grahame dies in France; Kenneth Grahame appears to be indifferent to the death. The year of Queen Victoria's Golden Jubilee is besmirched by the "Bloody Sunday" crackdown in Belfast.
1888	Grahame transfers to Chief Cashier's Office. His first pieces of prose, country essays, are accepted for publication in the *St. James's Gazette*.
1890	Grahame begins to contribute occasional essays on many subjects to the *Scots Observer* (which later becomes the *National Observer*).
1891	Grahame's "The Olympians" is published in the *National Observer*.
1893	Grahame's *Pagan Papers*, reprints of essays plus six new stories, is published. Women are admitted to work in the Bank of England.
1894	Grahame begins to contribute to *The Yellow Book*, an experimental magazine. His cousin, Anthony Hope [Hawkins] publishes the world-famous Ruritanian romance *The Prisoner of Zenda*.
1895	Grahame's *The Golden Age* is published; a review appearing in the *Daily Chronicle* by Algernon Swinburne, a prominent poet and critic, calls it "well-nigh too praiseworthy for praise." The trial of Oscar Wilde begins.
1896	The speed limit of 12 mph imposed on automobiles is rescinded.
1897	Grahame meets Elspeth Thompson. *The Yellow Book* ceases publication. Grahame's brother Roland marries.
1898	Grahame is appointed secretary of the Bank of England, one of the institution's three highest positions; he is one of the

Chronology

youngest men to occupy the post. In December he publishes *Dream Days*.

1899	Grahame marries Elspeth Thomson on 22 July.
1900	Alastair Grahame is born prematurely on 12 May with congenital cataract in his right eye (rendering it completely blind) and a squint in the left.
1903	A "wandering . . . lunatic" fires at Grahame in the Bank with a revolver.
1904	Grahame begins to tell his son the first of the stories that will develop into *The Wind in the Willows*.
1905	The speed limit for automobiles is raised to 20 mph.
1906	The Grahame family moves to Cookham Dene.
1907	Grahame writes letters to Alastair which contain a version of Toad's adventures. Grahame also entertains King George V's children at the Bank of England for tea.
1908	In June, Grahame resigns from the Bank of England on a relatively low pension of £400 per annum. *The Wind in the Reeds* is rejected by the American magazine *Everybody's* and a British publisher, The Bodley Head; however, Methuen publishes it under the title *The Wind in the Willows* in October.
1909	Theodore Roosevelt, the president of the United States, admires *The Wind in the Willows* and recommends the book to Charles Scribner.
1910	The Grahames move to the village of Blewbury, Berkshire, to the west of London. Grahame meets Roosevelt at Oxford.
1914	Alastair goes to the prestigious private ("public") Rugby School.
1915	Alastair transfers to Eton, another such prestigious school.
1916	Grahame publishes the *Cambridge Book of Poetry for Children*, in the Introduction to which he writes, "In the output of those writers who have deliberately written for children, it is surprising how largely the subject of *death* is found in bulk. Dead fathers and mothers, dead brothers and sisters, dead uncles and aunts, dead puppies and kittens, dead birds, dead flowers, dead dolls—a compiler of Obituary Verse for the delight of children could make a fine fat volume with little difficulty. I have turned off this mournful tap of tears as far as possible, preferring that children should read of the joy of life, rather than revel in sentimental thrills of imagined bereavement" (1916, vol. 1, pp. xiv–xv).

1918	Alastair goes to Oxford University.
1920	Alastair is killed by a train on 7 May, in what is almost certainly a suicide. Deeply affected, Grahame and his wife travel to Italy for eighteen months.
1924	On returning to England, the Grahames move to Church Cottage, Pangbourne, on the River Thames, twenty-five miles upriver from Cookham Dene, about fifty miles west of London.
1929	Grahame's brother Roland, with whom he had quarreled over money in 1913, dies; Grahame's reaction is not known.
1930	E. H. Shepard illustrates new edition of *The Wind in the Willows*. A. A. Milne writes *Toad of Toad Hall*.
1932	Grahame dies of cerebral hemorrhage on 6 July.

LITERARY AND
HISTORICAL CONTEXT

1

Historical Context

"Well, I mustn't be hard on you," said the Rat with forbearance. "You're new to it, and of course you don't know. The bank is so crowded nowadays that many people are moving away altogether. O no, it isn't what it used to be, at all." (9)

Kenneth Grahame was born into the secure world of Victorian England: the Queen had been on the throne for twenty-one years, and would remain on it for another forty-one years, until 1901. Britain's Empire, "on which the sun never sets," was at its height. Its currency and its financial institutions were strong and stable: its manufacturing industries made it "the workshop of the world." Power still lay with the old families, rooted in the land and agriculture; it was a male-dominated society, with a relatively static population.

In literary terms it was the era of the long novel of social realism; Dickens published *A Tale of Two Cities* in 1859 and *Great Expectations* in 1860–61; George Eliot published *Adam Bede* in 1859 and *The Mill on the Floss* in 1860; Anthony Trollope was at the height of his fame—*Barchester Towers* came out in 1857. The foremost poets of the time included Robert Browning (*The Ring and the Book*, 1868–69) and Alfred, Lord Tennyson (*Enoch Arden*, 1864).

But just as Grahame's childhood life was soon disrupted by the death of his mother and the disappearance of his father, so his life coincided with some of the greatest and most rapid social changes in British history. It is generally agreed by historians that the last two decades of the 19th century saw Britain in a state of social and literary flux. By the time Grahame published *The Wind in the Willows* in 1908, the stable world that he had known was under threat or actively disintegrating.

Britain, having fought the last "preindustrialized" war against Russian expansionism in the Crimea in 1854–56 (a war that revealed great military incompetence), was involved in another military disaster with the South African (Boer) wars of 1899–1902. Britain's superior forces were defeated; the war was unpopular at home, and in South Africa Britain was seen no longer as an imperial power with inalienable rights but as an oppressor. Some of the confidence of Empire was shaken. Throughout the first half of Grahame's life there was a succession of scares about impending war between Britain and France, Germany, Russia, and even the United States. At home, the education acts of 1870, which aimed to produce nationwide literacy, also carried with them the threat of social destabilization as the working classes expanded their intellectual horizons. Social unrest became a background theme to the period, and some historians have argued that this is linked to the fact that the extent of Britain's cultivated land fell by nearly half between 1870 and 1900.

Although Karl Marx's *Das Kapital* had no immediate political impact, it is perhaps symptomatic that the book was published in 1867. In active politics, the two great parties, Liberal and Conservative, gradually tried to placate the demands of the increasingly powerful working class and to attract their votes. The secret ballot was introduced in 1872, while the Trade Union Amendment Act of 1876 gave legal protection to trades unions for the first time, and there was increasing industrial unrest in the 1880s and 1890s. The middle classes were shaken by major strikes, such as the Dock Strike in London in 1889, and the Engineers' Strike of 1897. On the other hand, at the beginning of the century, a certain xenophobia, caused in part by an influx of cheap immigrant labor, led to the Aliens Act of 1905, which was supported by all classes.

These changes in industry were reflected in changes in the balance of political power. "Liberal socialism" became a force: in 1906, of the Labour Representation Committee's fifty-one candidates, twenty-nine won seats in the House of Commons, and the committee became the Labour Party (which remains one of the two main British political parties). Established in 1884, the Fabian Society, although socialist, was explicitly middle-class; writers such as George Bernard Shaw and H. G. Wells were associated with it. The Workers' Educational Association was founded in 1903 to bring education to the working man; Ruskin Hall was founded at the University of Oxford in 1899 for the education of working men, and 1896 saw the first popular daily paper, the *Daily Mail*. The radical Irish independence movement, Sinn Fein, was established at the end of the century.

As is all this were not disturbing enough, male dominance itself came under challenge. The women's movement began to acquire new and, if not effective, then disruptive force. The National Union of Women's Suffrage Societies was founded in 1897, but until 1914 was overshadowed in influence by the militant Woman's Social and Political Union (founded by Mrs. Pankhurst in 1903) and the Women's Freedom League (1908).

Not only was urban and industrial society changing, but the rural life that had come to symbolize stability was being destroyed. Suburbanization had begun around the big cities, especially London, with the building of the "tube" underground railway lines in the 1890s. The last of the mainline railways, the Great Central and Great Western Joint line from London to Birmingham, was completed in 1910, and along the railway lines new suburban areas were springing up in the Thames valley. The automobile, too, was changing the face of roads both urban and rural: it was suggesteed that these monsters should be preceded by a man with a red flag of warning when the speed restriction of 12 mph on motor cars was abolished in 1896; by 1905 the limit had risen to 20 mph.

All this meant the changing of a way of life, which was reflected in literature: the post-Romantic fashions of the Victorian age became more and more "precious" and, by Victorian standards, corrupt. The 1890s were the "decadent" years, epitomized by the outrageousness of Oscar Wilde, the pre-Raphaelites such as the Rossettis, and *The Yellow Book*, a dramatically experimental literary quarterly, founded in 1894 with Aubrey Beardsley as its art editor. There was a good deal of "bohemian" posturing, and both Kenneth Grahame and Arthur Ransome found themselves on the fringes of this society (very ably described in Arthur Ransome's 1907 book *Bohemia in London*). Not only did the writers of the day look "inward" but they also looked out to the countryside, to an arcadian past, and to an emerging neo-paganism. Manly outdoor activity was encouraged by a "muscular Christianity" movement; the nostalgia is exemplified by the founding of the Early English Text Society by Kenneth Grahame's friend F. J. Furnivall, and the frequent (and, to the modern reader, excruciatingly sensual and sentimental) appearances of the god Pan in print.

The novels of George Gissing (for example, *New Grub Street* [1891]) and Thomas Hardy (*Jude the Obscure* [1896]) focused on the realistic, the tragic, and the plight of the lower classes, but these tendencies were counterbalanced by a vigorous and witty popular literature that celebrated (with amiable satire) the new suburban culture. Notable writers in this genre were George and Weedon Grossmith with *The Diary of a Nobody* (1892) and Jerome K. Jerome with *Idle Thoughts of an Idle Fellow, Three Men in a Boat* (both 1889) and his magazine *The Idler* (1892). The atmosphere of the city was epitomized by Conan Doyle's "Sherlock Holmes" stories, while the paradoxes and richness and inherent mysticism of both city and country life was being celebrated by G. K. Chesterton, best known for his "Father Brown" detective stories.

But the man who wrote *The Wind in the Willows* must be set in yet another context—that of the development of children's literature. After two centuries in which children's books had been generally seen as the instruments of instruction, and in which fantasy had been seen as unworthy of *anyone's* attention, major changes took place in Kenneth Grahame's lifetime. Lewis Carroll's *Alice's Adventures in Wonderland* (1865) and Charles Kingsley's *The Water-Babies* (1863) were landmarks in establishing fantasy as a legitimate mode for children's books. *Alice*, especially, asserted the identity of the child, for whom the adult world seemed the arbitrary and irrational.

Over the next four decades, there was a rapid growth in children's literature, so much so that the period is frequently referred to as the "golden age" of British children's books. Fantasy continued to develop in the work of George MacDonald and Mrs. Molesworth, as did other genres—notably the traditional fairy tale, in collections by Andrew Lang (beginning with *The Blue Fairy Book*, 1889), and the animal fantasy of Beatrix Potter, whose classic *The Tale of Peter Rabbit* was published commercially in 1902. G. A. Henty, the greatest of the writers who celebrated the success of the British empire through stories for boys, began to write in 1880. Particularly influential in establishing an unpatronizing "narrative contract" between adult narrator and child reader was Edith Nesbit, while Rudyard Kipling, a master of most genres, celebrated England and Englishness (and the countryside) in a subtle and complex book, *Puck of Pook's Hill* (1906). All of this rich development took place in the context of childhood being more valued than ever before. Families became smaller, partly following the fashion set by royalty and partly from the rapid improvement in hygiene and medicine. One curious offshoot of this all was the "perfect child" cult, which took a view of childhood which was at once sentimental and patronizing. Its use, for example, of babytalk persisted well into the 1920s (A. A. Milne was a notable exponent).

Grahame's life, then, saw immense changes in all spheres, and yet he spent his working life in the Bank of England, at the symbolic stable center of the commercial world. His books, especially *The Wind in the Willows*, distill the reactions of an essentially conservative man, an outsider by virtue of his personal circumstances and his birth (he was a Scot), to a society whose traditional values were under threat.

His first works were sketches that emulated the "decadents" in a mild way, which were collected in *Pagan Papers* (1893). This book was generally a success, but he achieved real fame with his humorous sketches that looked back (and down) upon childhood: they were collected in *The Golden Age* (1895) and *Dream Days* (1898). These nostalgic and witty recollections, which were at least in part wish-fulfillment, exploited a dissonance between the innocent behavior of children and the sophisticated language used to describe it.

By the time that Grahame wrote *The Wind in the Willows*, his world, beneath its calm surface, was disintegrating. Quite apart from his personal tragedy of an unhappy marriage and a disabled son, his society itself was cracking. The Empire had been shown from without to be flawed, and within it the growing power of working classes and of women (particularly those of the middle and upper classes) were shaking the most stable social structures. There were rumors of war, and despite the riches in the Bank of England, Britain's power seemed to be in decline. More directly, the idyllic agrarian world was being overtaken, shattered, by the growth of suburbia and by the noise and pollution of the automobiles and railways. It was out of this profoundly changing world, and out of a man who felt himself to be displaced within it, that *The Wind in the Willows* emerges as a many-layered and allusive book.

2

The Importance of the Work

The country lay bare and entirely leafless around him, and he thought that he had never seen so far and so intimately into the insides of things as on that winter day when Nature was deep in her annual slumber and seemed to have kicked the clothes off. (43)

Notable among the many characteristics of great works of literature is the ability to show us, and to involve us in, two extremes: universal aspects of the human condition and specific, intimate aspects of one person. *The Wind in the Willows*, a "densely layered text fairly cluttered with second meanings,"[1] is remarkable in its ability to accomplish both these things, and to operate at many levels of meaning and symbol simultaneously.

Yet it is generally regarded as one of the most famous *children's books* ever written. Can a children's book actually carry such depths and subtleties? This is a question I shall explore in this book, for, quite apart from its unquestioned status as a British (and perhaps world) cultural artifact and literary classic, *The Wind in the Willows* also sits ambiguously on the boundary between literature for children and literature for adults. But in doing so—and this may be the secret of its success—it defines areas where the child's and the adult's imaginations coincide. Without doubt, the idyllic, irresponsible riverbank is an ideal playground for children, but it is also a nostalgic escape for the adult. To the young reader, the animals who inhabit it are comprehensible "types" of humanity who combine the freedom of childhood with some distinct advantages of adulthood. In the complex world of the adult reader, on the other hand, they represent comforting archetypes and, further, a class of adults—the rich and leisured—who retain many of childhood's advantages.

However, it is not sufficient to say that *The Wind in the Willows* can be read in two ways by two audiences: the two types of meaning interact positively, stemming as they do from deep inside one writer, and relating as they do to universal impulses. *The Wind in the Willows* is one of the few books generally classified as children's books to have joined the establish canon of English Literature. It has become a family classic, passed down from generation to generation—a part of the secret codes that, like the Badger's underground mansion, form the basic materials of culture. Writing twelve years after its publication, A. A. Milne described it in these prophetic terms:

> [I]t is what I call a Household Book. By a Household Book I mean a book which everyone in the household loves and quotes continually ever afterwards; a book which is read aloud to every new guest, and is regarded as the touchstone of his worth. But it is a book which makes you feel that, though everybody in the house loves it, it is only you who really appreciate it at its true value. . . .[2]

It seems clear that Grahame's book has the ability to generate enthusiasm over a lifetime, and to speak on many levels to many different kinds of audience. Similarly, although the book's setting and ambience is quintessentially English, it has developed an appeal far beyond the confines of its native land: it was much admired on its publication by Theodore Roosevelt, then the president of the United States, and by Alfred Deakin, the prime minister of Australia.[3]

The Importance of the Work

A good indication of the extent to which *The Wind in the Willows* has been assimilated into world culture is the way in which, as with a folk tale, each new generation remakes the book. A curious version of it, which combined characters from Washington Irving's *Sketch Book of Geoffrey Crayon* (1819–1820) with those from *The Wind in the Willows*, was called *Ichabod and Mr. Toad* (produced by Walt Disney in 1949[4]); and "Mr. Toad's Wild Ride" can still—or could until very recently—be found in California's Disneyland. *The Wind in the Willows* has appeared on radio and audio tape, on video and television, and in abridged, rewritten, and cartoon versions. New books have been written about its characters. In 1930 A. A. Milne, famous not only for his "Winnie-the-Pooh" books but probably the foremost London playwright of the time, wrote *Toad of Toad Hall*, a musical play for children which was produced successfully each year for more than forty years. A fifty-two-page version "retold for easy reading" was published in Britain in 1983, describing itself as "this most famous of all children's stories."[5] At the other literary extreme, a "countertext" was written, Jan Needle's *Wild Wood* (1981), which retells the story from the viewpoint of the stoats and weasels—in the confidence that its readers would be able to understands how it relates to *The Wind in the Willows*.

Beloved by children and adults alike, *The Wind in the Willows* has generated some interesting critical and theoretical discussion. Some of this has centered on one of the several paradoxes of the book—namely, that although the manners and mores are male, middle-class, and English, the fact that the characters wear (as it were) animal disguises brings an element of universality not simply across races but also across the divide between adults and children.

Although Kenneth Grahame was a famous author when he wrote *The Wind in the Willows*, his other books, when they are remembered at all, are remembered in its shadow. It is unlikely that his other work—but not at all unlikely that *The Wind in the Willows*—would have brought about two biographies of Grahame, the second of which, by Peter Green (1959), was reissued with lavish illustrations in 1982 as *Beyond the Wild Wood*. These books have been joined by a description, by Grahame's wife, of how *The Wind in the Willows* came to be written (*First Whispers of* "The Wind in the Willows" [1944]) and an exploration of Grahame's other works connected to "The Wind in the Willows" (*Paths to the River Bank: The Origins of "The Wind in the Willows"* [1983]).

The continuing commercial importance of the book is also illustrated by the fact that *The Wind in the Willows* continues to sell in very large numbers. When the British copyright expired in 1983, the book was immediately reissued by other publishers with new illustrations by artists such as John Burningham and Harry Hargreaves.

But, even more than a work of literature, whether for adults or children, it has become a cultural artifact. For a time in the 1980s, the English Tourist Board used the characters to attract tourists to "the real England"—the kind of arcadia that exists somewhere in the back of the mind of most adults in most countries.[6] *The Wind in the Willows* is, in a sense, important because it is important. But part of its fascination is its many layers and levels, and the way in which it presents us with a model for understanding how literature works. Margery Fisher, citing it in her *Classics for Children and Young People* says that it is "a book so tender and so full of bouncing humor, so wholehearted in the joy of living, that most of us return to it again and again to add to a permanent store of allusions and mental pictures."[7] It epitomizes the *adult's* idea of the children's book, at once a *bildungsroman*, a thriller, and a farce—all these things being made safe by strong images of home, place, security, and above all comedy.

The present work will explore all these aspects of *The Wind in the Willows*, necessarily from an adult point of view, but taking into account possible readings by children. As Lois Kuznets has observed, "The book has lasting appeal precisely because adults can argue about it and be interested enough to want to pass it on to their children by reading it with them."[8]

3

The Critical Reception

Mole drew his arm through Toad's, led him out into the open air, shoved him into a wicker chair, and made him tell him all his adventures from beginning to end, which Toad was only too willing to do. The Mole was a good listener, and Toad, with no one to check his statements or to criticize in an unfriendly spirit, rather let himself go. (221–22)

When *The Wind in the Willows* was first published, the majority of critics were disappointed, not because of what it was but because of what it was not. Kenneth Grahame had been a famous and much-admired writer *about* children, and here, it seemed, was a book *for* children—a tale about anthropomorphized animals, which had originated as a bedtime story. Where was the Olympian wit of *The Golden Age?*

Although *The Wind in the Willows* was an immediate success, essentially it was regarded as a children's books that adults could, with a little indulgence from their peers, themselves indulge in. The entry for Kenneth Grahame in the lordly *Oxford Companion to English Literature* expresses this status precisely:

> KENNETH GRAHAME (1859–1932), author of "The Golden Age" (1895), studies of childhood in an English countryside setting, which proved extremely popular. "Dream Days," a sequel, followed in 1898. *Grahame also wrote "The Wind in the Willows" (1908) a book for children which many of their elders have also enjoyed.* (My italics)[1]

The forms of treatment that *The Wind in the Willows* has received over time bear out the observation that serious critical attention to children's literature is a recent phenomenon. At the outset, the book's reception was at best puzzled.

The Golden Age and *Dream Days* are remarkable for being regarded as landmarks in the history of children's books without being children's books at all. *The Golden Age*, which elegantly and slyly recounts the doings of Harold and his siblings met with spectacular reviews, notably from the poet Swinburne ("well-nigh too praiseworthy for praise") and brought Grahame a worldwide reputation. In 1908 Grahame received a letter telling him that "in the Kaiser's cabin, on the royal yacht *Hohenzollern*, there are only two books in the English language. One of them is the Bible and the other is Kenneth Grahame's *The Golden Age*."[2] The book, together with its sequel, *Dream Days*, was also hugely successful in the United States; Grahame was asked to send the copies to the president, and on 20 June, 1907, Roosevelt replied, "I am sure that no-one to whom you could have sent these two volumes would appreciate them more than Mrs. Roosevelt and I. I think we could pass competitive examinations in them—especially in the psychology of Harold!"[3]

That American publishers rejected *The Wind in the Reeds*—as the book was called before it was noted that this was the title of a Yeats book—when Constance Smedley, the European representative of

Everybody's, sent the manuscript to them in 1907 suggests that the publishers assumed that the public, even after ten years, wanted more of the same. Indeed, the general public's reaction might well be summed up in the letter that Theodore Roosevelt wrote to Grahame, from the White House, on 17 January, 1909.

> My mind moves in ruts, as I suppose most minds do, and at first I could not reconcile myself to the change from the ever-delightful Harold and his associates, and so for some time I could not accept the toad, the mole, the water-rat and the badger as substitutes. . . . Then Mrs Roosevelt read it aloud to the younger children, and I listened now and then. Now I have read it and re-read it, and have come to accept the characters as old friends; and I am almost more fond of it than of your previous books.[4]

The reviewers, however, seem not to have reread it. The most important British newspaper, *The Times,* predicted that "Grown-up readers will find it monstrous and elusive, and children will hope, in vain, for more fun. Beneath the allegory ordinary life is depicted more or less closely, but certainly not very amusingly or searchingly." The reviewer then went on to deliver a remark that has become famous in the history of reviewing for its ineptness ("As a contribution to natural history, the work is negligible") and concluded by ignoring the book's originality altogether: "For ourselves we lay *The Wind in the Willows* reverently aside and again, for the hundredth time, take up *The Golden Age.*"[5]

If reviewers disappointedly agreed that this was not *The Golden Age* over again, they were also agreed that the book had several second meanings. The comic journal *Punch,* for example, while dismissing it as "a sort of irresponsible holiday story in which the chief characters are woodland animals, who are represented as enjoying most of the advantages of civilisation," went on to note that "Some grown-up readers may find in the story a satirical purpose which its author would probably disclaim."[6]

It was clear to many reviewers that the "animals" were not animals at all. The *Saturday Review of Literature* stated flatly that "His rat, toad and mole are very human in their behavior, and remind us of undergraduates of sporting proclivities."[7] H. L. Nevinson wrote in *Nation*, "All the animals had a very stirring time, and but for their peculiar shapes they would well pass for first-rate human boys."[8]

These opinions show clearly enough that, from the outset, the book's intended audience was unclear. Arnold Bennett, himself a distinguished realist novelist, concluded in *The New Age* that *The Wind in the Willows* was actually written for adults:

> The book is fairly certain to be misunderstood of the people. The publishers' own announcement describes it as "perhaps chiefly for youth," a description with which I disagree. The obtuse are capable of seeing in it nothing save a bread-and-butter imitation of *The Jungle Book*. . . . The author may call his chief characters the Rat, the Mole, the Toad,—they are human beings, and they are meant to be nothing but human beings. . . . The book is an urbane exercise in irony at the expense of the English character and of mankind. It is entirely successful.[9]

This line of thinking was taken up in the most favorable review, which appeared in *Vanity Fair*. Richard Middleton wrote:

> The book for me is notable for its intimate sympathy with Nature and for its delicate expression of emotions which I, probably in common with most people, had previously believed to be my exclusive property. When all is said the boastful, unstable Toad, the hospitable Water Rat, the shy, wise, childlike Badger, and the Mole with his pleasant habit of brave boyish impulse, are neither animals nor men, but are types of that deeper humanity which sways us all. . . . And if I may venture to describe as an allegory a work which critics, who ought to have known better, have dismissed as a fairy-story, it is certain that *The Wind in the Willows* is a wise book . . . just as young people read *The Pilgrim's Progress* and *Gulliver's Travels* for the story, so I fancy they will find Mr. Grahame's book a history of exciting adventures, and value it in this aspect no less than we, who find it a storehouse of glowing prose, gracious observation, delicate fantasy, and life-like and even humorous dialogue. . . . *The Wind in the Willows* is a fuller

book than [*The Golden Age* and *Dream Days*] and yet I believe
that Mr. Grahame has accomplished the harder task with no less
sureness of touch, with no less qualified a success.[10]

Had this view been accepted widely, the path traced by *The Wind
in the Willows* might have been very different indeed. Interestingly,
one reviewer who did recognize what critics would generally assume in
the following years—that this *was* in many senses a children's book—
derided that very fact. The reviewer, twenty-four years old at the time,
was to become as famous as Grahame, as a children's writer—Arthur
Ransome. Writing in the January 1909 issue of *The Bookman*,
Ransome wrote:

> *The Wind in the Willows* is an attempt to write for children
> instead of about them. But Mr. Grahame's past has been too
> strong for him. Instead of writing about children for grown-up
> people, he has written about animals for children. The difference
> is only in the names. He writes of the animals with the same wist-
> fulness with which he wrote of children, and, in his attitude
> towards his audience, he is quite unable to resist that appeal from
> dreamland to a knowledge of the world that makes the charm of
> all his books, and separates them from children's literature. The
> poems in the book are the only things really written for the nurs-
> ery, and the poems are very bad. If we judge the book by its aim,
> it is a failure, like a speech to Hottentots made in Chinese. And
> yet, for the Chinese, if by any accident there should happen to be
> one or two of them among the audience, the speech might be
> quite a success.[11]

One review of *The Wind in the Willows*, which appeared in the
Times Literary Supplement of 22 October, 1908—on the same page as
Virginia Woolf's (unsigned) review of E. M. Forster's *A Room with a
View*—gives us a clear picture of *The Wind in the Willows'* immediate
literary context.[12] That review grasped the importance of the book,
and for an interesting reason: apart from comparing it unfavorably
with its predecessors, it suggested that the book contained "the materials for an English 'Uncle Remus'"—which, insofar as the Uncle

Remus stories contain a good deal of social commentary, was quite perceptive.

After this the book, on its way to becoming a classic, received little critical attention. In 1930 the leading article in *The Times* could refer to *The Wind in the Willows* in a discussion of moleskin—indicating that the book had attained the popular status of a commonly understood reference point—but otherwise it had vanished from critical mention.[13]

The fact that the initial dispute about whether the book was for children remained unresolved seems, then, to have impeded critical appreciation of the book. The essential schizophrenia of the book was first explored in an essay that was not meant as criticism at all, the Introduction to A. A. Milne's highly successful stage adaptation of the book, *Toad of Toad Hall* (1929). Milne, as we have seen, was a great enthusiast of the book, and saw clearly that there were two kinds of book within it. "Of course," he writes, "I have left out all the best parts of the book; and for that, if he has any knowledge of the theatre, Mr. Grahame will thank me." The specific chapter of which he was thinking was "The Piper at the Gates of Dawn." Milne continues, "it seemed clear to me that Rat and Toad, Mole and Badger could only face the footlights with hope of success if they were content to amuse their audiences. There are both beauty and comedy in the book, but the beauty must be left to blossom there, for I, anyhow, shall not attempt to transplant it."[14]

As critical attention to children's literature developed, though, the ambivalence of the text became a primary concern. The critic Forest Reid, for example, excluded *The Wind in the Willows* from his list of good children's books: "*The Wind in the Willows* I shall not add; its sniggering sophistication rules it out."[15] In 1981 Elizabeth Cripps wrote an article for *Children's Literature in Education*, "Kenneth Grahame: Children's Author?," in which she remained ambivalent; in 1989 Mary Haynes wrote an article, "*The Wind in the Willows*—A Classic for Children?," in which she decided emphatically that it is a book for children.[16]

This question obtrudes itself even with critics who ostensibly are writing about other matters. W. W. Robson, discussing *The Wind in the Willows* in a book of critical essays which deals with the established canon, suggests that "its place in the literary canon is uncertain"—and so, by implication, is the kind of criticism it merits—because it does not fit into the approved categories of the "dominant literary orthodoxy." Equally, the difficulty over what kind of criticism is appropriate may be "partly due to the uncertainty about whether or not the book is children's literature."[17] Similarly, Humphrey Carpenter, in *Secret Gardens*, his important book on the "Golden Age" of children's literature, spends ten thousand words discussing every aspect of the book only to conclude that "*The Wind in the Willows* has nothing to do with childhood or children except that it can be enjoyed by the young, who thereby experience (though they do not rationally understand) what its author has to say, and are able to sense some of its resonances."[18]

Roger Lancelyn Green, a pioneering critic, agreed. He recalls that in Edith Nesbit's *The Wouldbegoods* (1901), the child's version of *Dream Days* as it were, the narrator Oswald Bastable—a boy much given to succinct literary criticism—comes across *The Golden Age*. Oswald observes that the book "is A1 except where it gets mixed up with grown-up nonsense" (chapter 5). Green goes on to point out that "*The Wind in the Willows* . . . is utterly different (though Oswald's criticism would be true of it, as there are a number of long passages where the story is held up for the sake of beautiful descriptive writing—some of the finest in recent literature, but certainly puzzling to most young readers)."[19]

So far, so good; criticism seemed to focus on enjoyment, both that of the reviewers and of the "real" readers. But from the 1950s and 1960s onward, children's literature became an academic preoccupation, and criticism, as it became more sophisticated and abstract, began to "use" the book in very different ways. Critics ceased to see the book in isolation, and the life and psychology of its author became a salient concern in assessing it. The reader's interpretation began to take precedence over any supposed (or even probable) intention of the author.

The first of these critical approaches saw *The Wind in the Willows* as a personal (and presumably unconscious) allegory. In a letter to Roosevelt, Grahame made a statement that has proved to be the starting point for much speculation. Writing of *The Wind in the Willows*, he asserted, "Its qualities, if any, are mostly negative—i.e.—

no problems, no sex, no second meaning—it is only an expression of the very simplest joys of life as lived by the simplest beings of a class that you are specially familiar with and will not misunderstand."[20]

In the first thorough examination of Grahame's life and writings, Peter Green's 1959 *Kenneth Grahame*, Green explored extensively this putative relationship between Grahame's life and the text. His conclusion is succinct: Grahame's claims of innocence were, he thought, "flagrantly untrue." He laid the foundations for other critics to explore the personal and social symbolism of the text with statements such as this:

> The social picture which *The Wind in the Willows* presents is not life as Grahame thought it was, or once had been: it is his ideal vision of what it *should* be, his dream of the true Golden Age. . . . The curious thing is that though Grahame set out to create a trouble-free Arcadia he could not stifle his private anxieties: the Wild Wood loomed menacingly across the River, stoats and weasels lurked ready to invade Toad's ancestral home.[21]

When he turns to the characters in *The Wind in the Willows*, Green sees them as aspects of the author's character. For example: "While condemning Toad's excesses, he has, one suspects, a sneaking urge to behave in exactly the same way: Toad, in fact, is a sublimation of all his own unrecognised desires, and is harried by all the forces which Grahame himself found particularly terrifying."[22] How legitimate one finds this kind of correlation depends on how far one thinks a book should be taken as an unfinished interaction between author, reader, and context. Some critics are in no doubt. Clifton Fadiman, for example, sees *The Wind in the Willows* as Grahame's revenge on "the adult world which he had been forced to join and on the century whose materialism his sensibility could not accept. He . . . was a confessional [writer]. The book that he stoutly protested he wrote for children was a letter written in invisible ink to himself."[23] Green is on the whole eclectic; later developments have been rather more polarized in their approach.

One of the earliest examples of such academic approaches appeared in the fledgling *Children's Literature* journal—then the

"Annual of the Modern Language Association Seminar on Children's Literature and the Children's Literature Association"—in Geraldine D. Poss's "An Epic in Arcadia: The Pastoral World of *The Wind in the Willows.*" Poss relates Grahame's literary experiences and awareness of the classical epic to the world he creates. It is an arcadia, but "Through his book Grahame weaves the gentler trappings of epic, dividing it into a classical twelve chapters, but omitting from the work all aspects of the heroic life that might cause strife and pain and eventually death." Poss's suggestion that this defusing of the epic structure relegates women to a "part of the wide world . . . which is kept forever separate from the enchanted circle on the river bank,"[24] is, of course, sound enough—but it is an abstract, literary approach that is far from the child reader.

In such criticism, certain themes reassert themselves, notably Grahame's links to the romantics: 1988 saw Lesley Willis's "'A Sadder and a Wiser Rat/He Rose the Morrow Morn': Echoes of the Romantics in Kenneth Grahame's *The Wind in the Willows*" appear in the *Children's Literature Association Quarterly*, and Richard Gillin's "Romantic Echoes in the Willows" in *Children's Literature.*[25] That examples could be multiplied attests to the way in which *The Wind in the Willows* is a prime text for academic dissection.

The basic premise of much of this "new" critical writing is that *The Wind in the Willows* is unquestionably a book worthy of study—although there is the occasional dissenting voice. Margaret Meek, a major British authority on reading, regards it as a blind spot: "Those who tell me they like the book, and many genuinely love it, praise the very features of it which give me a frisson of mild disgust." One of the features that least appealed to her as a child was what the characters stood for: "At no time did I want any of that male company; it represented too many kinds of social exclusions. Three bachelors of a certain (or rather, uncertain) age, free from any real responsibilities, spending their days messing about in boats, and gossiping about the intolerable social habits of Toad whom they consider to be their friend just made me embarrassed." And "the sentimental nonsense of the Piper at the Gates of Dawn put me off for years."[26] Hard words, but they provide a useful balance to the kind of criticism that stems totally from nostalgia.

In this book, I propose to take an eclectic approach: How does *The Wind in the Willows* work? How *can* it be read? What are its virtues for the child reader and the adult reader; the British reader and the non-British reader; the reader of 1908, the 1990s, the 2090s? And all this will focus on that central, paradoxical question: Just whose book *is* it?

A READING

4

Main Streams and Backwaters: Narrative and Structure

The Mole was bewitched, entranced, fascinated. By the side of the river he trotted as one trots, when very small, by the side of a man who holds one spellbound by exciting stories; and when tired at last, he sat on the bank, while the river still chattered on to him, a babbling procession of the best stories in the world. . . . (3)

THE SHAPES OF THE NARRATIVE

[T]he trees were thicker and more like each other than ever. There seemed to be no end to this wood, and no beginning, and no difference in it, and, worst of all, no way out. (52)

No traditional critical analysis can do justice to the complexity of *The Wind in the Willows*: we cannot separate structure from symbol,

symbol from character, or character from language. Its narrative structure reflects its symbolism, its symbolism is contained in its characters, its characters and their dialogue are made of language, and its language, in turn, parallels the narrative structure. Thus, if there is a good deal of overlap and interweaving in the present discussion, this in itself is an indirect tribute to the book.

It may be for this reason that one can only guess as to which part of the text is likely to strike the reader first or most forcefully. Perhaps what the characters seem on the surface or what they do are the things that we remember; reflections on symbolism might come later, or might register only subconsciously. Many readers might remember the anarchy of Mole or the gravity of Badger before they realize what these characters might mean. However, characters and actions exist only within a framework, and underlying the basic decisions that we make about whether the book is for us—for the adult or the child (or the child within us, perhaps)—is the *shape* of the book, its narrative structure.

The Wind in the Willows has a particularly fascinating structure; there is more than one kind of book here, and the same characters function differently in each one, and mean different things. Critics have not overlooked this. Jay Williams notes this basic point well: "Technically, Grahame's book shouldn't work. It appears to violate the primary canon of a book: unity. It is, in fact, three books pasted together, the adventures of Toad, the tale of the friendship of Rat and two prose-poems about the English countryside. Nevertheless, the book does play, as we used to say in show business."[1] Just how well it plays is another matter, though; as Humphrey Carpenter has noted, less charitably, "Though it is fine enough in structure, one feels that it is often shakily executed, and that the exercise could scarcely be repeated successfully, so near does it come to collapse."[2]

The simplest way of looking at the book is to identify its two basic narratives, Mole's story and Toad's story. The first narrative is peaceful and local, the second outgoing and violent; one critic has called them the centrifugal and centripetal plots.[3] The first, in its pace, reflectiveness, and seriousness, is more suited to adults than to children, whereas the second is farcical. The first is home, the second abroad; the first is slow and deep (as well as symbolic), the second fast and shallow (as well as funny). The two chapters that interrupt Toad's adventures, "The Piper at the Gates of Dawn," and "Wayfarers All" can be seen either as a counterpoint to the farce, or part of the reflective, centripetal, adult novel.

An exploration of certain ways one might read the structure of this book may give us some clue as to the responses that are possible: as Mole said of the countryside in winter: "He was glad he liked the country undecorated, hard, and stripped of its finery. He had got down to the bare bones of it, and they were fine and strong and simple" (43). Before we explore these bones, though, we can outline the theory that makes looking at them worthwhile.

It is well established that the human mind, especially in childhood, responds positively to "closure": it is easier and more comfortable to have a sense of ending or resolution in most tasks. This applies particularly to narrative. Broadly, there are three classes of story: those that return to where they began, or have normality and security restored to them; those that acknowledge the stable "center" of home, family, security, and yet move beyond it; and those that break completely away from this on an actual or symbolic level.

The first kind of story structure, the "closed" story, is very common in children's books: the child reader can enjoy vicarious excitement and yet return safely home. Classic examples are J. R. R. Tolkien's *The Hobbit* (with its significant subtitle, *Or There and Back Again*), or Arthur Ransome's *Swallows and Amazons*—but there are thousands upon thousands of others. This form is also common in lowbrow books that adults read below their intellectual capacity— romances and pulp novels, notably. This coincidence has led to some confusion in the minds of adults between the children's book and "poor" literature, and we may be able to detect just this confusion behind some of our reactions to *The Wind in the Willows*.

The second kind of story is what we might call the "semiclosed" story, *Bildungsroman*, or "growth-novel." Here, the characters begin at home, but develop through experience, so that they can move on or away in a significant way. Home may have an influence, but it serves essentially as something to be left behind. Books that take this shape are "developmental." They are for adolescents, perhaps: they posit confrontation with new experience rather than the confirmation of past experience. They are, in short, rather less comfortable: resolution is not total, security is not reconfirmed. Curiously, critics often have trouble coming to terms with such stories. This last concern is perhaps most relevant to *The Wind in the Willows*.

Tolkien again provides a good example of this type with Frodo's story in *The Lord of the Rings*; Frances Hodgson Burnett's *The Secret Garden* is another. Picturebooks, too, such as Rosemary Wells's *Timothy Goes to School* or *Benjamin and Tulip* show this basic pattern—which can cause further confusion. Books that *look like* books for children (notably picture books) are sometimes disconcerting in that they can have the "wrong" *narrative* shape.

The third kind of story is that with an unresolved ending or one in which very great changes or shifts have taken place in the course of the narrative. This is recognized as the "adult" narrative, a shape that allows us—indeed, forces us—to move on, as it were, ambivalently into the future. This shape acknowledges in a fundamental way the complexity of existence.

The dominance of the narrative shape in how we perceive stories can be demonstrated by various fantasy genres, and the folktales and fairy tales from which they derive. In folktales especially, the themes are profound, elemental, savage: they are often about wish-fulfillment, revenge, sex, yet they are now typically thought of as appropriate to children. The reason for this is, in part, that such stories very often come to a clear *resolution*—which is not what an essentially utilitarian western culture has trained its adults to recognize as significant. Stories that have ambivalent endings, on the other hand, such as the Russian tale retold by Arthur Ransome, "The Soldier and Death," have not been so easily assimilated into children's literature.

Often these several kinds of text exist side by side, uncomfortably. Mark Twain's *Adventures of Huckleberry Finn*, which is essentially a *Bildungsroman* of Huck overlaid with an adult novel about Jim the slave, collides in the last chapters with the resolution-seeking children's book character of Tom Sawyer. In *The Lord of the Rings*, Sam Gamgee's plot is of the first type, Frodo's of the second, the elves' and men's of the third. In P. L. Travers's *Mary Poppins* there is a clash between the children's resolving stories and Mary's unresolved (and unresolvable) adult story. Small wonder such books find it difficult to find a niche in the literary hierarchy: they seem on their surface to be one thing, but a very different level makes its presence known as we read them.

The Wind in the Willows exemplifies all these questions about narrative, and it is clear that what narrative means to us is interrelated with the symbolism of its characters. A good example may be found in a series of stories contemporaneous with *The Wind in the Willows*, one that may well have influenced it—the Sherlock Holmes stories by Sir Arthur Conan Doyle.

Although intended for, and primarily read by adults, these stories have been appreciated by children and adolescents (they are currently available in Britain in several editions designed for the "junior" market). Whatever their content in terms of dealing with horror or murder, almost all of the stories are of the first of our narrative types: there is resolution, which is reinforced by the very powerful symbols of the omnipotent, almost godlike Holmes and the comfortable lodgings of Baker Street, which contrast with the threatening, fog-filled London. Whatever adult problems are "out there," we, standing beside the childlike Dr. Watson, can be confident and comfortable in the knowledge that we can return home unharmed. Of course, the Sherlock Holmes stories are not considered to be "great literature"— and, of course, they *cannot* be, given that "greatness" (or "adultness") is commonly associated with a certain plot shape. To enjoy Sherlock Holmes, therefore, involves responding to secure narratives, to gratify "childish" impulses.

And so it is with *The Wind in the Willows*. For Dr. Watson, read Mole; for Holmes read the Water Rat (who is wise to the ways of the river); for the London underworld, read the Wild Wood. The parallels are valid: although *The Wind in the Willows* and the Holmes stories speak both to adults and to children, their status is held to be questionable.

In this respect, though, *The Wind in the Willows* is more complex: it provokes multiple responses, because the narrative shapes require such responses. If certain parts of the book are "for adults," then, we might be able to identify these by tracing the various shapes in the book.

One way of identifying the shapes is to consider "external" evidence: How was the book written? For this we can turn to the research surrounding *The Wind in the Willows*.

SHAPING THE BOOK

> Mole drew his arm through Toad's, led him out into the open air, shoved him into a wicker chair, and made him tell him his adventures from beginning to end. . . . Toad, with no one to check his statements or to criticise in an unfriendly spirit, rather let himself go. (222–23)

It is significant that the story of how *The Wind in the Willows* came to be written must be unraveled from the accounts of his wife Elspeth and of his first biographer, Patrick Chalmers. It seems clear from the evidence that Grahame's marriage was not a happy one, and he spent a good deal of time abroad or otherwise away from his family. Equally, Elspeth Grahame, perhaps as a disappointed reaction to her husband's behavior, seems to have put a vast amount of emotional energy into convincing herself that Alastair was a remarkable child. (This pressure may well have led to what was almost certainly his suicide while at Oxford University.) Grahame is said to have told his small son bedtime stories, one of which was reported to Elspeth by her maid, when she was asked, before a dinner party, where her husband was. The maid replied, "Oh, he is up in the night-nursery, telling Master Mouse [Alastair] some [story] or other about a toad." Elspeth later elaborated this story, most improbably, with eavesdroppings. Grahame also wrote a short piece about a pig, "Bertie's Escapade," which was "published" in a small magazine that Alastair and a friend produced. Elspeth described it as "really a sort of rehearsal for *The Wind in the Willows*."[4]

In the summer of 1907, Grahame stayed in London while Alastair and his mother remained at their home in Cookham Dene (within commuting distance of London) or were on holiday. Grahame wrote a series of letters that contain most of Toad's adventures—a small part of chapter 6 and a good deal of the material that appears in chapters 8, 10, 11, and 12. He supplemented this by asking Alastair what he remembered of the bedtime stories and by getting Miss Stott, the governess, to quiz him.[5] The earliest surviving original letter gives some clue to how Grahame worked. It is dated 10 May 1907.

My Darling Mouse,

This is a birth-day letter to wish you very many happy returns of the day. I wish we could have been all together, but we shall meet again soon, & then we shall have *treats* . . . Have you heard about the Toad? He was never taken prisoner by brigands after all. It was all a horrid low trick of his. He wrote that letter himself—the letter saying that a hundred pounds must be put in the hollow tree. And he got out of the window early one morning, & went off to a town called Buggleton & went to the Red Lion Hotel & there he found a party that had just motored down from London, & while they were having breakfast he went into the stable-yard and found their motor car & went off in it without even saying Poop-poop! And now he has vanished & every one is looking for him, including the police. I fear he is a bad low animal.[6]

The letters make curious reading, in that, from 17 July, when Grahame is writing about Toad's encounter with the Gipsy (in what became chapter 10), the letters become only a serial—that is, there are no greetings or personal comments to Alastair; as David Gooderson points out, "the boy's letters . . . contain resentment at his parents' frequent absences. He missed them, appealing to them individually and together . . . to come and see him." Most of the appeals seem to have been in vain.[7]

The letters "to" Alastair form the backbone of this part of the book, and Grahame revised them carefully. Compare, for example, these passages from the letters and from the published chapter 8, "Toad's Adventures." The letters read:

> Then the gaoler's daughter went & fetched a cup of hot tea and some very hot buttered toast, cut thick, very brown on both sides, with the butter running through the holes in it in great golden drops like honey. When the toad smelt the buttered toast he sat up & dried his eyes for he was exceedingly fond of buttered toast; & the gaoler's daughter comforted him. . . .

The published text is far more sensuous:

> When the girl returned, some hours later, she carried a tray, with a cup of fragrant tea steaming on it; and a plate piled up with very hot buttered toast, cut thick, very brown on both sides, with the butter running through the holes in it in great golden drops, like honey from the honeycomb. The smell of that buttered toast simply talked to Toad, and with no uncertain voice; talked of warm kitchens, of breakfasts on bright frosty mornings, of cosy parlour firesides on winter evenings, when one's ramble was over and slippered feet were propped on the fender; of the purring of contented cats, and the twitter of sleepy canaries. (136–37)

As Lois Kuznets has pointed out, many of these changes are "self-reflexive and not all of them readily accessible to the child reader."[8] Grahame has built up the narrative, and in doing so, has accentuated the symbolic and allusive content.

Beyond this, we know that "The Piper at the Gates of Dawn" and "Wayfarers All" were "written separately and later inserted into the draft,"[9] but there is no evidence as to when the first five chapters were written—nor why or at what point they were inserted into the manuscript. Peter Haining has suggested that "Wayfarers All," "the most quoted chapter in the book," was presaged by an essay that Grahame had written for *The Yellow Book* in July 1895, called "The

Wanderer." In this, the writer walks along the sand listening to the tales of a London businessman who has had "the rare courage . . . to kick the board over and declare against further play."[10] "The Piper at the Gates of Dawn," on the other hand, is clearly similar in its celebration of quasi mysticism to a hundred other pieces written around this time.

This curious process, in which the making of two thirds of the book, of two of the narratives, is unchronicled, even by Elspeth Grahame, is highly suggestive. First, is it clear that Toad's adventures, initially *for* a child, subtly altered their narrative shape and allusiveness as they developed. Second, those parts of the narrative which are not mentioned in the account of how *The Wind in the Willows* came to be written are in fact, as we shall see, the very personal *Bildungsroman* elements of Mole's story and the mystic or escapist *adult* interpolations. In a very important sense, recognizing the different narrative shapes unlocks the secrets of both the intent and intended audience of *The Wind in the Willows*.

FROM THE RIVER BANK TO DULCE DOMUM

Spring was moving in the air above and in the earth below and around him, penetrating even his dark and lowly little house with its spirit of divine discontent and longing. (1)

Grahame knew his classics well, and in some senses he was writing an epic. *The Wind in the Willows* is divided into twelve chapters in the classical manner—one of which is called "The Return of Ulysses"—and parts of Toad's adventures parody the *Odyssey*. However, the direct resemblance of the book as a whole ends there; it is, rather, the first five chapters that form, as it were, a mini-epic, a complete story in themselves, a complete narrative section. Within this section some of the rules of epic are followed. More important, these first chapters contain the narrative shapes that I discussed earlier.

We begin with the Mole, the central subject—in a useful technical term, the "focalizer" of most of this section: we focus on him, looking over his head as his adventures unfold, seeing things from his point of view, observing what he observes. The narrator may be omniscient, but "he" introduces his world from Mole's angle.

In chapter 1, the story starts in the middle of Mole's spring cleaning: Mole leaves home, a significant escape in narrative terms, and comes up from his underground drudgery into the sunlight (we shall return to the multiple symbolism here). He rambles and meanders away from his home, comes to the River, meets the Water Rat, and in one breathless sweep he is initiated into a new world, a new society: like Bilbo Baggins, Huck Finn, Laura Ingalls, or Alice, a new world has opened up, and for the time being there is no looking back. And it is all very gentle and easy: as the Water Rat says, "'Look here! If you've really nothing else on hand this morning, supposing we drop down the river together, and have a long day of it?'" (6–7).

The narrative now does two things: it develops Mole's change in life, and—for Grahame was nothing if not a very careful craftsman—it introduces motifs and characters that are going to recur and, despite its warring elements, give the whole book cohesion. These include the River, food, the Wild Wood ("'O that's just the Wild Wood,' said the Rat shortly. 'We don't go there very much, we riverbankers'" [9]), and new friends: Badger ("H'm! Company" [13]), Otter ("Proud, I'm sure" [13]) and, of course, Toad ("It's all the same whatever he takes up; he gets tired of it, and starts on something fresh." [14]).

By the end of the chapter, then, Mole has moved from one life to another; indeed, he has changed *homes*. There has been a moment of truth, a moment of danger, when he overreaches himself and falls foul of the River. But, as with many children's stories, security is immediately reinforced by all kinds of comforting symbols. The wording at the end of the chapter is significant:

> When they got *home*, the Rat made a *bright fire* in the *parlour*, and *planted* the Mole in an armchair in front of it, having fetched down *a dressing-gown* and slippers for him, and told him river *stories* till *suppertime*. (19; emphasis added)

This whole chapter, because of its structure (leaving home, being initiated, finding a new home) introduces us to the overall structure of Mole's *Bildungsroman*. Although he has moved on, there is plenty of compensating psychological *closure* for the characters and the reader—the warmth, the cozy words and images. How far what we have seen can be read as escape by adults or as comfortably bounded adventure by children, we shall consider later.

In chapter 2, "The Open road," Mole is still the narrative's focalizer, and it is in relation to him that we first encounter Toad. (This is worth remembering, for the chapters that feature Toad are sometimes lumped together as if together they had a kind of unity.) "The Open Road" might be seen as a prelude to the later adventures, but it is Toad observed, not Toad accompanied: it is Toad the eccentric, judged by conservative norms, not Toad the rebel judged by his own standards.

The chapter begins firmly on the riverbank, where Rat is sitting, composing a song; this is the secure home, set on a "bright summer morning" surrounded by friends. Rat and Mole, safe in their two-animal boat, set out on an adventure, by degrees: first they visit Toad's house, and then they travel in a substitute home, Toad's "canary-coloured cart." Like the incident with the gipsy in chapter 10, this cart (or caravan) may well have been inspired by one of Grahame's favorite books—indeed, one of the inspirational books of the nostalgic-country movement—George Borrow's *Lavengro* (1851). This, one of Borrow's three fantastic-autobiographical books (the others were *The Bible in Spain* [1843] and *The Romany Rye* [1857]), romanticized the idea of the gipsy/Romany, and held great appeal for citybound people such as Grahame. In *The Wind in the Willows*, he celebrated Borrow's freedom of spirit, not only in the caravan but in the character of Toad.

Toad conducts a mild running battle against Rat's devotion to his river, and he manipulates Mole's divided loyalties between his new way of life and an even newer one. As the narrator reflects, in an interesting comment upon both Mole and Grahame:

> Poor Mole! The Life Adventurous was so new a thing to him, and so thrilling; and this fresh aspect of it was so tempting; and he had fallen in love at first sight with the canary-coloured cart and all its little fitments. (29)

Thus, the means of transport which Toad adopts, for all the sardonic tones with which his friends regard it, is in keeping with the quiet rural ways and Mole's quiet progress. In this respect, it is significant that for two days they "ramble over grassy downs and along narrow by-lanes . . . across country by narrow lanes," and it is only when they reach "their first high road" that disaster—in Mole's terms—strikes. Indeed, so secure is Mole's place in the scheme of things now that the Rat discounts Toad, and talks "exclusively to Mole" (39).

As might be expected, this excitement and displacement—indeed, destruction of a way of life—requires a strong closure, and sure enough, Rat and Mole deposit Toad at Toad Hall and return, in keeping with the circular narrative, to where they began.

> Then they got out their boat from the boat-house, sculled down the river home, and at a very late hour sat down to supper *in their own cosy riverside parlour*, to the Rat's great joy and contentment. (39; emphasis added)

The chapter ends, as it began, on the riverbank, with with Mole now pursing that most secure and well-documented of pastimes, fishing. In the first chapter, Mole had moved on a little, but home was reasserted. In the second chapter, there is the classic shape of the children's story: home-adventure-home. With the next two chapters, the pattern changes again.

The idea of Badger and the Wild Wood had been established in the first chapter, and Mole's adventure of chapter 3 is presaged in a sinister way with Mole finding "his thoughts dwelling again with much persistence on the solitary grey Badger, who lived his own life by himself, in his hole in the middle of the Wild Wood" (41). The radical disturbances of this chapter also begin with a very strong evocation of "the pageant of the river bank," in a passage no less purple than the loosestrife featured on the riverbank: all is secure, all is ordered. Yet the Mole, in a moment of pride or, more classically, hubris, "slips out" to go to the Wild Wood alone, and approaches his nadir, the low point of his existence. Everything in the Wild Wood is the opposite of the riverbank house—cold, dark, threatening, and uncertain. In the exact middle of chapter 3, in the exact middle of this first group of five chapters, we find Mole thoroughly defeated: the child who has disobeyed his elders or, alternatively, the innocent adult who has disobeyed the expert. Grahame leaves no effect untried in his buildup to the "Terror"; Mole has retreated into a hollow tree, itself a poor mockery of the security he has given up.

> He was too tired to run any further and could only snuggle down into the dry leaves which had drifted into the hollow and hope he was safe for the time. And as he lay there panting and trembling, and listened to the whistlings and patterings outside, he knew it at last, in all its fullness, that dread thing which other little dwellers in field and hedgerow had encountered here, and known as their darkest moment—that thing which the Rat had vainly tried to shield him from—the Terror of the Wild Wood! (47)

More unsettling still is the fact that the narrative *leaves* Mole there. For the first time in the book, the narrator's attention abandons Mole; he is stripped even of the strength of his centrality. The limits of the innocent/child have been reached, and a superior power is needed. That superior power is the new focalizer, the Rat, who grimly and efficiently arms himself according to the necessary rules and confronts the Wild Wood—and defeats it: "the whistling and pattering, which he had heard quite plainly on his first entry, died away and ceased, and all was very still" (48). Clearly, Rat is an insider, one who knows "passwords, and signs, and sayings which have power," and accordingly he brings comfort and sleep to Mole. However, Rat serves here as a brother figure rather than as a father figure: when even he is almost defeated by the snow, an even greater power is needed to restore confidence. Chapter 3 ends, as it were, on the brink of closure, on the brink of security, as Rat and Mole hammer on Badger's door.

From the depths of the cold Wild Wood to the security of Badger's house is a short step, and in some editions, a drawing by Ernest H. Shepard contrasts, on the left, Rat and Mole in the snow, and on the right the rich glow from Badger's kitchen. From this point, in the epic scheme of *The Wind in the Willows*, everything is, for Mole, upwards. Not only are his physical wants provided for and his bruised ego massaged, but he is admitted into an even more exclusive society—Badger's—which, literally and figuratively, underlies the rest of the world. (The illustration by Shepard emphasizes this even more; whereas in the text, Mole and Rat follow Badger "down a long, gloomy, and, to tell the truth, decidedly shabby passage" (60), Shepard pictures a hall with a draped coatrack, a walking stick, and a barometer—all comfortable symbols of British middle-class life.)

Structurally, this opening scene of chapter 4 counterbalances the depths of misery to which Mole (and Rat) had sunk. Symbolically, it is much more: indeed, of all the symbols in children's literature, the kitchen is among the most potent (this will be discussed in more detail in chapter six). The episode at Badger's is a long, low-key episode, enclosed and full of comforts. Mole's bedroom is half full of winter stores of food, and the following morning's breakfast is lavish—and involves buttered toast, a nursery delight that crops up again in Toad's adventures. The Terrors of the Wild Wood are further tamed by the appearance of the lost hedgehogs, to whom Mole and Rat can feel superior, and by the domesticating idea that there are schools for hedgehogs out there—and, further still, by the appearance of the fearless Otter.

Mole is also initiated into the underground society, whose strengths could hardly be more explicitly stated; as Mole says: "Once well underground . . . you know exactly where you are. Nothing can happen to you, and nothing can get at you. You're entirely your own master" (70). (There must be a good many of us who have found a similar comfort—and not only as children—under the blankets on the day before some distasteful experience. John Moore, the distinguished English country writer, several of whose books owe various debts to *The Wind in the Willows*, uses a similar device in his *Dance and Skylark* [1951].[11])

It is when Mole and his friends at last set out for the riverbank home that the lack of closure of the chapter reveals how Mole has moved on. Compared with the ending of chapter 3, this is a positive rather than a negative lack of closure. Otter ("as knowing all the paths" [76]) guides them back across the frozen fields, and the contrast between what is behind them and what is before them is described very strongly: behind them "they saw the whole mass of the Wild Wood, dense, menacing, compact, grimly set in a vast white surroundings; simultaneously they turned and made swiftly for home, for firelight and the familiar things it played on . . ." (86). And though the chapter ends before they get there—we are left with Mole "eagerly anticipating the moment when he would be at home again among the things he knew and liked" (76)—this implied but uncompleted closure ends on a soothing note.

Arthur Ransome uses the same device, although on a larger scale, in his "Swallows and Amazons" series (1930–1948), the displacement from "home" increasing with each book, so that *Swallows and Amazons* (1930) begins and ends with the same characters at the same place, whereas *Great Northern* (1948) begins and ends far from home, without even the main characters "on stage." Grahame, in *The Wind in the Willows*, skillfully manipulates the changes in narrative structure, between the different parts of a single book.

Yet the riverbank, of course, is not Mole's home at all, and chapter 5, the final chapter of this group, complements the first. In it, Mole moves backward, from being part of his new society to revisiting his old, and in doing so closes this independent part of the book. Of course, this closure also integrates the new (Rat and all he brings) with the old; just as Mole came into Rat's home, so Rat comes into Mole's. The fact that the final focalizer of the chapter is Mole, tucked up in bed, is balanced by the fact that Rat, the facilitator, is nearby.

As with the other chapters, there is a contrastive structure in chapter 5, "Dulce Domum." The scenes at the beginning, with the companionable Mole and Rat making their way home past the huddled sheep in the frosty air, contrast home and away, inside and outside: Mole and Rat watch people in the warm houses of the village, from the outside—and, ironically, the bored caged bird. In the middle of the chapter, at Mole End, they are in a "cheerless . . . long-neglected house" (87): by the end of it, Mole is rolled up snugly in his blankets looking "round his old room, mellow in the glow of the firelight that played or rested on familiar and friendly things which had long been unconsciously a part of him" (96).

Leaving aside any other implications, this is the structure that brings, in effect, Mole's story to a close. He has been out into the world, he has matured, as each chapter has shown, and he is now home again; he has grown up and can now take the world or leave it. Under the guidance of the Rat, he is able to accept his place both in his new world and his old. As a piece of psychology, it embodies a familiar pattern as people grow up and away from their origins; and though it might seem to be optimistically simple, or (as I shall argue later) disconcertingly restrictive, there is no doubt that the message speaks to a large audience. The Mole "saw clearly how plain and simple—how narrow, even—it all was; but clearly, too, how much it all meant to him, and the special value of some such anchorage in one's existence" (96).

This, then, is the secret narrative of *The Wind in the Willows*, whose origins are uncertain, which speaks to elements in both the adult and the child—the circle of home and experience: of finding new paths and reconciling them with old places. But if Mole's story is universal in one way, Toad's may be in another, even though on the surface it might seem that it is now time for the farce to begin.

"THE WORLD HAS HELD GREAT HEROES"

"Now, Toady, I don't want to give you pain, after all you've been through already; but seriously, don't you see what an awful ass you've been making of yourself?" (201)

In chapter 6 there are some very marked changes—from deep winter to early summer, from evening to morning, from Mole's home to Rat's, from rest to preparatory activity. There is also a marked change of pace. In the stories involving Toad there are many more scenes and characters than in Mole's story—and as many again in that than in "Wayfarers All" and "The Piper at the Gates of Dawn." The latter of these, which for all intents and purposes has only two characters in it, and unity of time and very nearly of place, is bounded by two chapters that leap across time, place, and a multiplicity of characters.

It is generally agreed that the impression of irresponsible action is sustained in Toad's adventures, although this presents certain theoretical difficulties. To describe narrative, as Jonathan Culler has put it, we must decide what actually constitutes an *event*. Is it a change of place, characters, dialogue . . . ? Culler suggested that we need to characterize events (or "plotemes," by analogy with phonemes) as "culturally marked significant actions. . . . What the reader is looking for in a plot is a passage from one state to another—passage to which he can assign thematic value. . . ."[12]

Although more interesting from the viewpoint of fantasy and social symbolism, Toad's adventures have their own structural logic. They can be seen either as three chapters (for most of which Toad serves as the focalizer) which almost invert Mole's progress, or as five chapters that have a circularity of plot, moving from home to home. What is most striking from the viewpoint of the structural coherence of *The Wind in the Willows* is that time and again, Toad's story reflects and parodies Moles: far from being uneasy partners, these two plots reflect each other.

In "Mr. Toad," "Toad's Adventures" (chapter 8), and "The Further Adventures of Toad" (chapter 10) Toad is at first seen from the outside, as his friends gather to reform him. Like the Mole, he escapes the shackles of convention, although his movement from Toad Hall is downward rather than upward—indeed, it is difficult not to stumble over symbolism at almost every turn! Like Mole, Toad rambles away from his life irresponsibly, but instead of joining an established society such as that of the riverbank, he joins the new, symbolized by the automobile. (There is, indeed, a literal collision between old and new, between cart and car!) In doing so, he crosses the divide between two kinds of fantasy world, from that of the animals to that of the humans—a change so radical that Grahame, as we shall see, is forced to use not quasi realism (for example, that of the riverbank) but a grotesque pantomime world. The chapter ends with Toad, famously, "a helpless prisoner in the remotest dungeon of the best-guarded keep of the stoutest castle in all the length and breadth of

Merry England" (117). For all that it is made safe by humor, it is a nightmare of sorts, the opposite of Mole's happy haven at Rat's house. And at that point, at the peak of the verbal excitement and the depths of Toad's despair, there is a pause, and the book shifts radically to the long, sustained prose-poem of "The Piper at the Gates of Dawn"—as far from high farce as one could imagine.

In "The Paper at the Gates of Dawn" we see a celebration of "insiderism". Moreover, important from the viewpoint of the narrative, Mole takes a small but stolid part in it: he is elevated to, and totally absorbed into, this safe world of a mystical, adult pattern. The anarchic child that is Toad is placed very firmly in the proper scheme of things.

The next chapter, "Toad's Adventures," is the first that is truly Toad's own, and the farce is resumed. After another escape and another chase, it ends with Toad again displaced, and, like Mole, taking refuge in a hollow tree—although he doesn't suffer from Mole's tortured insomnia: "At last, cold, hungry, and tired out, he sought the shelter of a hollow tree, where with branches and dead leaves he made himself as comfortable a bed as he could, and slept soundly till the morning" (153).

In terms of Toad's adventures, this unresolved chapter end brings us to a parody of home; in terms of the whole book, it parodies the structure that we have seen before. The incidents may well be farcical, not to be taken seriously, but the underlying narrative pattern is doing something more serious: it is moving Toad on through the same developmental cycle we saw with Mole. This may well seem to be taking the farcical character of Toad altogether too seriously—but the reader may well be making sense of the whole book through the parallels in the narratives.

Again, from this relatively carefree level, we move to the mesmeric atmosphere of chapter 9, "Wayfarers All," and here the chief significance is again the role that Mole plays. Now he is not simply the "young friend" of Rat: he is a positive influence in sustaining the status quo. It is he who applies to Rat a doctrine that Rat had given him in the first chapter: "'beyond the Wild Wood comes the Wide World,' said the Rat, 'And that's something that doesn't matter, either to you or me. I've never been there, and I'm never going, nor you either, if you've got any sense at all'" (10). Now that the Rat, mesmerized, wishes to do just that, Mole, by his lyrical description of the joys of home (and we have already seen that he did not regard himself as a poet) helps to "cure" Rat of this wayward madness. The implication is that Mole has become a complete insider: no longer an acolyte of the Rat, his status is secure.

Not so Toad, though: alternating between triumph and catastrophe, he careers on his way, through chapter 8, surviving the most awkward of all the human-animal encounters (with the barge-woman) and parodying Borrow's *Lavengro* in his meeting with the gipsy. If "Wayfarers All" is written from Grahame's firsthand experience of the Mediterranean and his inner longings, "The Further Adventures of Toad" draws rather more on literary antecedents—among them, again, parody. The last time we saw Toad on a common (in England, an open area of rough grazing land, which anyone can use), it was in company with Mole and Rat, the horse grazing beside the canary-colored cart and "a yellow moon, appearing suddenly and silently from nowhere in particular, came to keep them company and listen to their talk" (31). This time, however, there is hot sunshine, and both the common and the gipsy are regarded with a singular lack of romanticism, and with a startling allusion to the very thing that is taboo in Mole's world:

> He looked about him and found he was on a wide common, dotted with patches of gorse and bramble as far as he could see. Near him stood a dingy gipsy caravan, and beside it a man was sitting on a bucket turned upside down, very busy smoking and staring into the wide world. (186)

Just as Mole's escape from the terrors of the Wild Wood is celebrated by the meal in Badger's secure kitchen, so Toad's escape is, parodically, celebrated by "wild" food. Whereas the meal that Mole eats is very symbolic and unspecific, the meal that Toad "takes on board" is very specific, indeed, very literary food. The "hot rich . . . most beautiful stew in the world, being made of partridges, and pheasants, and chickens, and hares, and rabbits, and peahens, and guinea-fowls, and one or two other things" is very reminiscent of the Irish stew concocted by Harris, George, and "J" in Jerome K. Jerome's *Three Men in a Boat* (a book I shall consider in more detail in chapter 7). That stew was also made of "one or two other things": "here was a dish with a new flavour, with a taste like nothing else on earth . . . and as for the gravy, it was a poem—a little too rich, perhaps, for a weak stomach, but nutritious."[13]

The end of Toad's adventures in the "outside" world demonstrates Grahame's narrative technique. The automobile, the very same one, reappears; Toad is again swaggering through the countryside—and at the last, at the close of chapter 10, he finds himself under the eye of Rat again. And it could hardly be overlooked that this encounter with Rat (198) is expressed in virtually the same words as was Mole's first encounter with the Rat (4). When Mole first saw that twinkle in the depths of the hole it meant a new freedom, but for Toad it means captivity: to both—although, as we shall see, this is suppressed in the text—it means repression.

The two-chapter coda that follows, "'Like Summer Tempests Came His Tears'" and "The Return of Ulysses," chapters 11 and 12, could be seen as completing Toad's odyssey, with its climactic battle and his return to home and possible accession to adulthood. This is an attractive view, and one that could be sustained theoretically—indeed, one that probably subsists at the back of many readers' minds. However, in terms of narrative technique, it must be pointed out that the focus is less and less on Toad, and the narration tends to view the actions more abstractly.

Thus Toad is now put firmly in his place as the errant child of the book: it is Mole and Badger who have been suffering, and it is Mole who is regarded as Badger's most trusty lieutenant:

> Toad felt rather hurt that the Badger didn't say pleasant things to him, as he had to the Mole. . . .
>
> "Excellent and deserving animal!" said the Badger, his mouth full of chicken and trifle. "Now, there's just one more thing I want you to do, Mole, before you sit down to your supper along of us; and I wouldn't trouble you only I know I can trust you to see a thing done,

and I wish I could say the same of every one I know. I'd send the Rat,
if he wasn't a poet . . . I'm very pleased with you, Mole!" (229–30)

By shifting his point of view from Toad as focalizer to Mole as
focalizer, Grahame harmonizes the two apparently opposing (but actually complementary) elements in the book—the structures of conservatism and anarchy, of various kinds of experience. Thus the book
ends on a note of stability and unity. Mole is grown up, having proved
himself in many different ways, and Toad has been civilized and has, in
his fashion, grown up too: "After this climax, the four animals continued to lead their lives . . . in great joy and contentment" (240). On the
course that brings us to this point two stories have been blended
together: at the beginning it is Mole who is shy of the important Mr.
Toad, but by the end the positions, if not actually reversed, are consid-
erably altered. As we have seen, though, the stories are also symbioti-
cally related, each reverberating off the other. Thus, the dismissive
tone that Roger Sale has adopted is difficult to justify: "The book must
end lamely since a chastened Toad is of no interest; and the unchas-
tened Toad has too many tales told of him already."[14]

BRANCHING STREAMS:
OTHER READINGS OF THE NARRATIVE

Their old haunts greeted them again in other raiment, as if they had
slipped away and put on this pure new apparel and come quietly
back, smiling as they shyly waited to see if they would be recognized
again under it. (122–23)

The above discussion, of course, is not the only way to read the text,
although it is generally agreed that there are two stories. It is possible
to conjecture, as Neil Philip does, that "for Grahame Mole, not Toad,
was the book's protagonist is proved by one of his suggested titles, for-

tunately unused, *Mr Mole and His Mates.*"[15] The fact that Toad's story is generally considered to be inferior to Mole's is a central issue in the critics' battle for the book; however, it is debatable whether this position amounts to the colonization of a children's book by adults or, rather, to the rescue of an adult's book by casting its lesser parts into perspective. Humphrey Carpenter is generally dismissive of the comedy of Toad's story: "But this idiom was not Grahame's *forte* and he does not seem very comfortable in it."[16] Such a comment seems to overlook some of the greatest moments of farce in the English language—Toad and the Bargewoman, Toad in the court of law, or Toad hijacking the automobile—as well as their significance as counterpoints to the other parts of the book.

To counteract this tendency to downgrade half of the book, Michael Mendelson argues that the text can in fact be considered as a whole, and "instead of separating the two stories and devaluing one" he prefers to examine "how Grahame not only juxtaposes but interlaces" his two different plots. Mendelson sees a constant dialectic between responsibility and romance: Mole's adventurous spirit is moderated by the steady life of the riverbank; Toad's adventurous spirit is seen in contrast to the values of the riverbank's dwellers. He also points out that there is a seasonal element in the book which reinforces the subtle parallelisms and counterthemes. For example, the change of season between high summer and winter in chapter 3 presents us with a question: "The answer, of course, is that while nature may be sequential, art is patterned and thematic. We skip seasons here in order to develop through the Mole the temperate chord of natural instinct rather than the discord of extravagant impulse."[17]

Similarly, with the arrival at Badger's house, "the call of adventure" is juxtaposed with "the lure of home."[18] This is a persuasive argument, for parallelism is clear throughout the text: at almost every point, Grahame is working an art of contrasts that overrides any narrative disunity. Thus there is, underlying the book—as an symbolic substratum—the idea of the eternal seasons, with which Rat but not Toad is in accord. In this structuring of the book, the two stories "finally dovetail" when Rat rescues Toad; from that point on, "the two stories continue to coalesce, as the reunited friends resolve to retake Toad Hall . . . a consolidating motive that will call up heroic adventurism in the service of the pastoral home."[19]

At this point, the narrative structure coalesces with the ideological-political one. But the importance of considering the underlying narrative structures is clear—as is the fact that a reader may well recognize and react to several structures simultaneously. As Sarah Gilead has noted:

> Much children's literature . . . dramatises conflict between a child-realm and an adult-realm, without being able to settle conceptually in either one. "Childhood" may be lost in the past and retrievable only through distorting adult fantasy, wish, or memory; "adulthood" may be intolerably weighted with frustration and loss. But it is rare to find these issues dramatized in the interaction between two rival plot lines and in their alternate narrative perspectives. In Grahame's novel, we find the narrative structure itself made metaphor for the psychocultural conflicts within the characters, the work as a whole, and perhaps the literary genre which that work exemplifies.[20]

5

Natural History: Characters, Animals, and Personal Symbolism

"Go on, Ratty," he murmured presently; "tell me all. The worst is over. I am an animal again." (218)

THE MEANING OF THE ANIMALS

The Mole knew well that it is quite against animal-etiquette to dwell on possible trouble ahead, or even to allude to it. . . . (11)

The Wind in the Willows began life as a story for Grahame's son, Alastair. This has led some (perhaps rather romantic) critics, to assume that it has a special status as a children's book; after all, other great children's books—notably, *Alice's Adventures in Wonderland*, Kipling's *Just So Stories*, C. S. Lewis's *The Lion, the Witch and the Wardrobe*, and

J. R. R. Tolkien's *The Hobbit*—also began as stories for specific children. But it should also be borne in mind, as Clifton Fadiman rather brutally put it, that "The sordid fact is that to be a good writer of juveniles you don't have to love children, any more than you have to love criminals to write *Crime and Punishment*."[1] Roald Dahl may have written *Charlie and the Chocolate Factory* for his disabled son, but that has not stopped critics from perceiving all manner of unpleasantness in the book. The biggest-selling British children's author in history, Enid Blyton, who was at one time considered to be the "mother of the world's children," actually had a very poor relationship with her own.

In fact, Grahame, like Carroll and Lewis, was thoroughly ambivalent about children and childhood; as Humphrey Carpenter has observed, he wrote during "the upsurge of introspective, non-realistic writing for children in Britain."[2] "Introspective" is the key word here: the relationship that many adults have with childhood is quite curious in that one of the first critical assumptions they make is that writers are really writing for themselves. To evaluate children's books, critics have needed to see them as something other than books for children: in order to be significant they must be about a person, and the only available "serious" person involved seems to be the writer. Arthur Ransome sums up the matter succinctly, although his argument tends to cast writing for children as being positive in itself.

> It is true that some of the best children's books were written with a particular audience in view—*Alice in Wonderland* and *The Wind in the Willows*, for example. Many others were not, and it is impossible to read even those that were without realizing that one member of that audience, and the one whose taste had dictatorial rights, was the author. Lewis Carroll was not "writing down" further than to Lewis Carroll, and though Kenneth Grahame could count on a delighted listener in his small son, the first person to enjoy the exquisite fun of Mr Toad and his friends was Kenneth Grahame himself.[3]

If we are to take a children's book seriously, the argument runs, then, as with any other book, we must tease out its hidden meanings—analyze what it says and be alert to what it does not say. This is a respectable enough proposition when a book is about an author's peers; but when, like *The Wind in the Willows*, it seems to be about talking animals, the critical process enters a further area of confusion.

What, then, does Grahame mean by using animals in *The Wind in the Willows*? On the surface, anthropomorphism, and the kind of empathy which relates to animals in this way—animism—is a characteristic of childhood, and adults consequently approach such books with caution. Indeed, to approach them at all, adults must read them as allegorical or symbolic—as *The Wind in the Willows* was read by its first reviewers. Even books with such obvious adult satirical purposes as Swift's *Gulliver's Travels* or Orwell's *Animal Farm* can find themselves in limbo; similarly, serious studies of philosophy such as Russell Hoban's *The Mouse and His Child* need a good deal of special pleading because of what they appear to be. As W. W. Robson said of *The Wind in the Willows*, the main feature of the animal device, "at least as far as the older child or adult reader is concerned, is that it cuts off the possibility of the book's being read other than symbolically."[4]

The animal story is rooted in the earliest folklore: among the very first printed books were editions of *Aesop's Fables*, and animals were seen as natural analogs to the human world. But since the rationalist movements of the eighteenth century—and, indeed, until very recently—fantasy has been neither fashionable nor respected in the adult literary world, whatever the judgment of the marketplace, and, with rare exceptions, animal stories have gravitated toward the nursery.

There, they hold certain advantages for the storyteller. First, the use of animals avoids problems of race and racism—although this depends upon how you feel about the animals that are regarded as villains: "political correctness" decrees that we should at least give the Big Bad Wolf the benefit of the doubt. Second, a good deal of the narrative relies on actual or proverbial animal characteristics, that is, characteristics seen as similar to human characteristics: owls are wise, mice timid, pigs greedy, donkeys miserable, and so on and so forth. Similarly, just as fantasy worlds generally simplify character and reduce moral issues to their simplest basic forms, so a single example of a species can stand for all: it doesn't matter that there is only one donkey, one piglet, or one Rat, Mole, Badger, or Toad in the story.

The animal story, then, like the fairy story, finds itself part of children's literature by accident, and it does not really belong there. It is another example of the confusion between the necessary element of the childlike in human nature, and the fear of the *childish*. It can convey a great deal of meaning in a very economical way, a great deal of richness, but it carries as well the risk of being misunderstood. *The Wind in the Willows* is perhaps the most extreme example of this trend.

Why did Grahame write about animals? He himself said:

> As for animals, I wrote about the most familiar and domestic in *The Wind in the Willows* because I felt a duty to them as a friend. Every animal, by instinct, lives according to his nature. Thereby he lives wisely, and betters the tradition of mankind. No animal is ever tempted to belie his nature. No animal, in other words, knows how to tell a lie. Every animal is honest. Every animal is straightforward. Every animal is true—and is, therefore, according to his nature, both beautiful and good. I like most of my friends among the animals more than I like most of my friends among mankind.[5]

All that is, of course, very idyllic—and he was writing an idyll. It is also almost entirely beside the point. Margaret Blount sums this up well: "For animals, read chaps, and highly unusual chaps they are. . . . The animals are middle-aged men living in what must be early retirement, earning nothing . . . doing nothing as becomes animals. . . . Yet there is a fascination in seeing what the adult animals, given a limitless holiday, are doing."[6] As Jay Williams has suggested, "the book can hardly be called a fantasy. It is, rather, a series of stories about a group of interesting people who just happen to be rather out of the ordinary—I suppose 'eccentric' is the word."[7]

There is something Moleish, perhaps, about Mole, something Badgerish about Badger: he certainly sleeps in the winter a good deal. But are toads ebullient, or rats artistic? Certainly, stoats, weasels, and ferrets are vicious in their way—but then otters can be as well. For the most part, after the first chapter Grahame ignores his characters' "animal nature." There, Otter is at one moment a country gentleman contemplating a riverside picnic, at the next a real otter, chasing mayflies. Badger is at one second a real badger, rooting under a hedge and trotting forward, the next an elderly gentleman who "hates Society."

Generally speaking, Grahame's handling of this duality in his animals is masterly, and, as we have seen, he is careful to remove any interaction with humans into the realm of farce. But he does make "mistakes," as when in the first chapter Rat is rowing the Mole on the river:

> "I like your clothes awfully, old chap," he remarked after some half an hour or so had passed. "I'm going to get a black velvet smoking suit myself some day, as soon as I can afford it." (8)

Elsewhere, their animalness, as it were, is significant only in terms of size or scale, and then only to illustrators. Toad is the only animal to encounter humans face to face—and, as we shall see, Grahame solved his problems there very dexterously. A. A. Milne has made the key point very well:

> In reading [*The Wind in the Willows*], it is necessary to think of Mole, for instance, sometimes as an actual mole, sometimes as a mole in human clothes, sometimes as a mole grown to human size, sometimes walking on two legs, sometimes on four. He is a mole, he isn't a mole. What is he? I don't know. And, not being a matter-of-fact person, I don't mind.[8]

But why did Grahame take on these difficulties, however ingeniously they could be solved, when he could simply have written about humans? Naomi Lewis may well have found the answer, in linking *The Wind in the Willows* to Grahame's earlier books. *The Golden Age* and its sequel were an invocation of childhood, based upon Grahame's very clear memories—but, she notes, "The child-theme of *The Golden Age* and *Dream Days* was, for Grahame, played out; all five children at the end of the tale were already moving towards the Olympian world.

Yet animal comrades, neither old nor young, free both from child-hood's rules and adult burdens (like under-graduates) exactly fitted the need."[9]

As we have seen in considering the narrative, the need is for characters capable of taking on the dual role of child *and* child-in-adult; animals can do so where no realistic human character could have. Yet they also serve other purposes, as Margaret Meek, not a sympathizer, has pointed out very bluntly: "To meet them is to encounter the same person, the author, variously disguised as a Rat, a Mole, a Badger and a Toad, all equally egocentric and self-regarding. Pity."[10]

If the riverbank is Grahame's ideal world, then the riverbankers (surely a mild pun, Grahame being a London banker) may indeed represent him, or forms of what he wished himself to be.

Although Meek's view is widely accepted, it is far from being the only one; indeed, one of the fascinations of *The Wind in the Willows* lies in the fact that its characters have so many facets. Not only are they Grahame's ideals, the people he would like to be, the people he values, but they are also his fears: the people he would like to meet but perhaps dares not.

Biographically inclined critics might suggest that Grahame was disappointed at not having attended Oxford or pursuing an academic career, which would have allowed him to mix with the moneyed, the leisured, and the intellectual; hence *The Wind in the Willows* could be seen as his dream. Although this thesis rests upon the assumptions that Mole is Grahame's primary alter ego, and that the other characters exist only in relation to him, it can coexist with the idea that all the animals show some aspects of his character. If there is something of Grahame in all the animal characters, it is not surprising that there are some remarkable complex interactions—notably between Rat and Mole: while we are clearly intended to sympathize with both of them, there are occasions when Rat is clearly patronizing Mole and exposing his weaknesses.

More than most aspects of *The Wind in the Willows*, the question of how the characters are to be interpreted shows the critics at odds with each other. To begin with, there is the question of class. Are the characters "neo-Georgian social types"[11]—and, if so, types of what? Here we enter the minefield of the English social class system, which is difficult and subtle enough for insiders but incomprehensible to outsiders, and there is disagreement as to the social status—let alone the ages, sizes, and narrative functions—of the characters. What can be made of all this?

THE FAMOUS MR. MOLE

[T]he Mole saw clearly that he was an animal of tilled field and hedgerow, linked to the ploughed furrow, the frequented pasture . . . For others the asperities . . . that went with Nature in the rough; he must be wise, must keep to the pleasant places in which his lines were laid and which held adventure enough, in their way, to last for a lifetime. (76)

Let us begin, as the book does, with the Mole, and the first words he says: can we ignore the "possible *class* implications of '*Up we go!*'"— or the psychological and symbolic fact that, as W. W. Robson points out, *The Wind in the Willows* begins in exactly the opposite fashion to *Alice's Adventures in Wonderland*, which has Alice fall *down* the hole.[12] Alice's exploration is inward, the Mole's is outward. And, once Mole emerges into the critical sunlight, what do the critics see? Mary Haynes suggests that "At the beginning he is a rather naive, middle-aged, perhaps rather *lower* middle-class bachelor";[13] Fred Inglis sees him as a "middle-aged recluse emerging as a practical administrator-soldier";[14] and Margaret Blount describes him as "the childlike Mole."[15] So far so good—middle-aged but childlike—until we come to A. A. Milne's thoughts about transposing him onto the stage: "Rat and Mole [should be] young and slender. Indeed Mole might be played by some boyish young actress."[16]

This confusion is not really surprising. On the one hand, Mole is cast in the role of the innocent. He is irresponsible and impetuous;

he is impulsive and wildly enthusiastic ("Oh My! Oh, My!"), and a lover of warmth and comfort. He is, in fact, the innocent eye through which we can regard the adult world—which is usually taken to be the child's eye.

But although Mole may have childlike characteristics, he is clearly an adult—specifically a (relatively) lower-class clerk. (Arthur Rackham portrayed him in this way, giving him clerkly spectacles.) Some readers have found his model in a best-selling book of the period, George and Weedon Grossmith's *The Diary of a Nobody* in which the city clerk, Mr. Pooter, is mercilessly though sympathetically satirized. He begins his diary

> My dear wife Carrie and I have just been a week in our new house, "The Laurels," Brickfield Terrace, Holloway—a nice six-roomed residence, not counting basement, with a front breakfast-parlour. We have a little front garden; and there is a flight of ten steps up to the front door, which, by-the-by, we keep locked with the chain up.

When the Pooters buy some items to decorate their house, Mr. Pooter describes them thus: "some pretty blue-wool mats to stand vases on . . . a pair of stags' heads made of plaster-of-Paris and coloured brown. They will look just the thing for our little hall, and give it style; the heads are excellent imitations."[17] Mr. Pooter, though out of his depth in the modern world, is an honest, simple man, and it is not difficult to see the resemblance between "The Laurels" and "Mole End."

"Mole End," which the Mole is spring-cleaning as *The Wind in the Willows* opens, has "a sort of fore-court," of course, and "On the walls hung wire baskets with ferns in them, alternating with brackets carrying plaster statuary—Garibaldi and the infant Samuel, and Queen Victoria, and other heroes of modern Italy. . . . In the middle was a small round pond containing goldfish and surrounded by a cockle-shell border. Out of the centre of the pond rose a fanciful erection clothed in more cockle-shells and topped by a large silvered glass ball that reflected everything all wrong *and had a very pleasing effect*" (92–93; emphasis added). It is difficult not to read this as a rather patronizing description by the narrator (or, possibly, the Rat, as he is the "person present" to whom the fore-court is being revealed). The way in which Rat praises the Mole's house—"the jolliest little place I ever was in"—or his choice of beer—"*Sensible* mole!"—lends some weight to this interpretation. The final comment, one assumes, comes to us through Mole's consciousness—and clearly contradicts notions of what would be appropriate to an upper-middle-class house. Mole, then, is of the people. Is Grahame mocking himself, or perhaps only the other aspiring clerks—or is he attempting to be supportive of his alter ego? The innocent figure of Mole starts to take on some interesting ramifications.

And so Mole goes into the world—and his first meeting with Rat involves a social solecism.

> "Would you like to come over?" inquired the Rat presently.
> "Oh, it's all very well to *talk*," said the Mole rather pettishly, he being new to a river and riverside life and its ways. (5)

Mole in his innocence, fails to see that he is being gently patronized by his considerate host. Not only is Mole described as not knowing much, but there are some things that he will never know—what the riverbank once was, for it has become "so crowded nowadays. . . . it isn't what it used to be, at all" (9). Despite what some critics suggest, there is also a difference in age, or perhaps merely in experience, as when Rat says to Mole over the question of rowing, "Not yet, my young friend . . . wait till you've had a few lessons. It's not as easy as it looks" (17).

If we pursue the idea of Mole as Grahame, then his befriending by Rat is not an unreasonable bond, and as Robson observes, "Mole is Sancho Panza, Dr. Watson to Rat's Sherlock Holmes."[18] Mole has an accepting attitude, and in a sense, Mole and Rat are complimentary aspects of Grahame himself. Humphrey Carpenter observes,

> On this level, Rat and Mole are not simply the apprentice and the experienced artist, but different facets of the same artistic mind. Mole is by turns timorous and rash, while Rat alternates between

dreamer and practical man-of-the-world. One begins gradually to feel that Mole is the artist's personality as human being (he closely resembles many aspects of Kenneth Grahame himself), while Rat is an expression of the two sides of an artist's actual work: inspiration . . . and craftsmanship.[19]

In this first chapter, then, Mole's awkwardness is treated with a certain kindness. In this respect, Mole's first meeting with Otter is of particular interest. Although I shall focus on the question of language in the next chapter, it is worthwhile to anticipate it at this point.

Little critical attention has been given to Otter, but in his few appearances his role is clearly established. He turns up in the Wild Wood, unafraid of anyone and "knowing all the paths" (76); he appears obliquely in "The Piper at the Gates of Dawn" as a worried parent, and he has a walk-on part at Toad's final party, where it is difficult not to see him in an immaculate dinner jacket. Although Inglis thinks that the four main characters "translate readily" into the suave clubland heroes of the superior thriller-writers of the day, John Buchan and "Sapper," as well as into those of P. G. Wodehouse"[20]—a view that the character of Otter certainly might well be seen as substantiating—it seems as though Grahame saw him not as middle-class but as genuinely upper-class. Were the passing hedgehogs to call him "my Lord," one would not be surprised.

Had Grahame achieved his ambition of studying at Oxford University, he might well have rubbed shoulders with the nobility; as Secretary of the Bank of England, he would undoubtedly have made their acquaintance on business matters. (On one occasion he entertained the king's children at the bank.) However, there is a very great difference between making someone's acquaintance and being his or her friend, being accepted into an "inner circle."

So the question turns to how Grahame describes the "friendship" between Mole and Otter; the answer can only be evasively. As we shall see, Grahame's uses language as a mask as much as a means of communication, and this meeting is a classic example. Otter appears at the scene of the picnic:

"Greedy beggars!" he observed, making for the provender. "Why
didn't you invite me, Ratty?"

"This was an impromptu affair," explained the Rat. "By the
way—my friend Mr. Mole."

"Proud, I'm sure," said the Otter, and the two animals were
friends forthwith. (13)

Certainly, when next they meet, in Badger's house, Otter is friendly,
but his greeting has a certain dismissive air about it. Mole should know
his place, friendship or not: "Here, Mole, fry me some slices of ham,
like the good little chap you are. I'm frightfully hungry, and I've got
any amount to say to Ratty here. Haven't seen him for an age." Mole,
of course, *does* know his place (which is at least slightly above that of
the hedgehogs): "So the good-natured Mole, having cut some slices of
ham, set the hedgehogs to fry it, and returned to his own breakfast,
while the Otter and the Rat, their heads together, eagerly talked river-
shop. . ." (69).

The Mole, then is accepted into this desirable society, but only
on limited terms, initially at least. Later on, he is absorbed into it,
becoming a respected member who is at once Rat's friend and confi-
dant, Badger's most trusted lieutenant, and Toad's equal in arms. To
explore these facets of Mole's "meaning," though, we can go no further without considering Mole's other new friend, the Water Rat.

THE GALLANT WATER RAT

"I'd send the Rat, if he wasn't a poet." (230)

It seems a little pedantic to point out, as Patrick Chalmers does, that
the Rat is probably actually a Water Vole (the latter presumably was
rejected because it rhymes with Mole a little too easily).[21] The Rat has
given rise to as many conflicting critical descriptions as has Mole, from
"schizophrenic" (Blount) to "soldier-poet" (Inglis).[22] His age is uncer-

tain; he has the air sometimes of an undergraduate, sometimes—indeed, more often—of a leisurely wealthy person of impeccable breeding, in his late twenties. He certainly has some help around the house: when Toad returns from his initial attempts to regain Toad Hall he hears "the chink of dishes on a tray" [210]; in short, apart from being a rat, he is a poetically minded bachelor insider of independent means, of the kind that Grahame himself aspired to be.

This status is certainly beyond Mole's ambition; as Carpenter says, when Mole meets Rat "there is a suggestion that here is someone subtly his social superior, who leads a leisured gentlemanly existence while Mole is a creature of routine, who inhabits a more lowly home."[23]

There has also been some interesting speculation about Rat's origins, apart from being simply a wish-fulfillment figure. Carpenter and Prichard suggest that he is "based on an amalgam of Grahame's friends Frederick Furnivall and Edward Atkinson."[24] In literary terms, one source (or perhaps merely a parallel) for Water Rat may be a character in Oscar Wilde's book of fairy and moral tales, *The Happy Prince and Other Stories* (1888). Grahame was on the periphery of Wildean society, and it is difficult to imagine that he did not know this book. Wilde's story "The Devoted Friend" is a parable, cast in the form of the folktale, of selfishness masquerading as friendship. The tale is told on the bank of a pond, by a linnet to a water rat, and the opening may remind us not merely of the Water Rat of *The Wind in the Willows* but also of his friends, the ducks, and also (ironically) the Mole's attitude toward society:

> One morning the old Water-rat put his head out of his hole. He had bright beady eyes and stiff grey whiskers, and his tail was like a long bit of black indiarubber. The little ducks were swimming about in the pond . . . and their mother . . . was trying to teach them how to stand on their heads in the water.
> "You will never be in the best society unless you can stand on your heads," she kept saying to them. . . . But. . . . [t]hey were so young that they did not know what an advantage it is to be in society at all.

The Water-rat also asserts very strongly his concept of friendship—
which again brings us to *The Wind in the Willows*, with its emphasis on
comradeship and the giving of symbolic gifts—when he says: "I am not
a family man. In fact, I have never been married, and I never intend to
be. Love is all very well in its way, but friendship is much higher.
Indeed, I know of nothing in the world that is either nobler or rarer
than a devoted friendship."[25] The moral of the story is that a friendship
that is patronizing is ultimately false—and in this context it is interesting to consider the subtext of Rat's relationship with Mole. Although
there seems little doubt that Rat is intended to be an admirable character, this is not necessarily what consistently strikes the reader: there is
an element of repression, even of suffocation, about his relationship
with Mole, and it is only toward the end of the book that Mole escapes
from it by becoming Badger's first lieutenant. Whether or not Mole is
Grahame in fur, he is certainly searching not only for a new life but also
for a mentor—a brother or father figure. Because this tendency, to look
for approbation and authority, is a more or less universal characteristic
of childhood, we are presented with another paradox of *The Wind in
the Willows*. A basic assumption about children's books is that they
should be developmental in some way, even if, as we have seen, experience is made safe by closure: the older the implied audience, the more
the books should be "confrontational" rather than "confirmatory." Yet
it is in the *limiting* of Mole's education, primarily by his "friend" the
Rat, that *The Wind in the Willows* declares itself to be more a regressive
book for adults than a progressive one for children.

Curiously, this repression/regression first occurs almost immediately after Mole has made his break for freedom. The two animals are
rowing down the river when Mole inquires first about the Wild Wood
and then:

> "And beyond the Wild Wood again," he asked: "Where it's all
> blue and dim, and one sees what may be hills or perhaps they
> mayn't, and something like the smoke of towns, or is it only
> cloud-drift?"
> "Beyond the Wild Wood comes the Wide World," said the
> Rat. "And that's something that doesn't matter, either to you or

me. I've never been there, and I'm never going, nor you either, if you've got any sense at all. Don't ever refer to it again, please." (10)

The river is "my world, and I don't want any other" (9), and Mole is expected to accept this, more or less, as the price of friendship. Rat maintains this theme throughout the first adventure with Toad, and Mole, somewhat reluctantly, perhaps, follows along:

> "Mole's going to stick to me and do as I do, aren't you, Mole?"
> "Of course I am," said the Mole loyally. "I'll always stick to you, Rat, and what you say is to be—has got to be. All the same, it sounds as if it might have been—well, rather fun, you know!" (29)

(Rat's success in "taming" Mole can be seen in chapter 9, when Mole stops him from leaving for the "wide world.") Grahame stresses that the Rat is kindhearted, and "hated disappointing people, and he was fond of the Mole" (29), and so they go on the expedition, even though Rat keeps up a kind of mild moral blackmail by thinking about his river all the time. The fact that Rat knows of old that Toad's fads do not last long might perhaps rob this episode of some of its altruism—but it is clear that here, for all his friendship, he is in control.

Similarly, when Rat saves Mole from his adventures in the Wild Wood, he emphasizes that only insiders such as himself know the survival codes. Later, his authority is temporarily displaced by Badger's authority and camaraderie with the subterranean Mole, but Rat is soon able to put Mole down, as we have seen, by talking shop about the river with Otter.

All of this does suggest that Grahame's attitude toward the class to which he aspired was more ambivalent than some commentators have suggested. But Mole certainly accepts Rat's message, and sees the "error of his ways" in the light of his Wild Wood experience. As they are returning home (that is, to Rat's home), Mole soliloquizes what is an essentially restrictive philosophy, one that, though Grahame perhaps partly shared it, is a little surprising in a children's book ostensibly written to stress adventure:

Mole saw clearly that he was an animal of tilled field and
hedgerow, linked to the ploughed furrow, the frequented pasture,
the lane of evening lingerings, the cultivated garden-plot. For others . . . Nature in the rough; he *must be wise*, must keep to the
pleasant places in which his lines were laid and which held adventure enough, *in their way* to last for a lifetime. (76; emphasis
added)

These seem to be very quietistic, resigned phrases—and this kind
of homily is repeated at the end of "Dulce Domum," when Mole accepts
that "it was good to think that he had this to come back to" (96). Two
things are blurred over at this point; first, that "the larger stage" to
which "he must return" is in fact a place constricted by Rat's imagination and ambitions; and second, that "He was now in just the frame of
mind that the tactful Rat had quietly worked to bring about in him."

The Rat's role in "Dulce Domum," the chapter in which Mole
formulates his philosophy of life, is therefore rather suspect. Some
commentators have found the chapter to be an uncomfortable experience. The image of the Mole failing to communicate to the Rat (or
the Rat failing to understand) is a scene of a type very basic to many
children's books, and the desolation of the snow merely emphasizes
this. Yet Mole's "paroxysm of grief" (perhaps a slightly extreme reaction?) leads Rat to assert his authority: he becomes not only a force-
ful elder brother but a superior being, and the fact that the narrative
focuses more on the Rat than on the Mole emphasizes this superiority. Equally, it might be agreed that Mole's sense of loss could be
Grahame's—hence the strength of the reaction. This view could be
supported by the unusually intrusive comment by the narrator on the
insensitivity of humans: "We other, who have long lost the more subtle physical senses . . . " The use of "we" perhaps disguises the
anguished "I."

The visit to "Mole End," with Rat initially trying to cheer Mole
up, becomes both a nostalgic celebration of an England that probably
never was (with the field mice taking the part of the local peasantry)
and an act of slumming. Rat manipulates the Mole, and the Mole is
reduced to being ineffectual, not to say dimwitted. As Margaret Meek

puts it, "the implication being that Rat's tact made up for Mole's bad taste, when in fact Mole's lack of subtlety is exposed quite cruelly."[26] As we have seen, this is a double-edged sword: the more that Rat takes control, the more demeaned is Mole. It is almost as if Grahame has ceased to sympathize with Mole.

One is reminded of Oscar Wilde's story; perhaps this kind of friendship is not as admirable as the book attempts to make out.

Rat, though, finds his own nadir in the later chapters "Mr. Toad" and "Wayfarers All," first when Toad makes a fool of him ("even the Mole, though he took his friend's side as far as possible, could not help saying, 'You've been a bit of a duffer this time, Ratty!'" [110]), and later when he is nearly seduced away to the degenerate south.

"Wayfarers All" shows, in animal terms, one side of the cycle of the seasons: "The Rat was a self-sufficing sort of animal, rooted to the land, and whoever went, he stayed; still, he could not help noticing what was in the air, and feeling some of its influence in his bones" (155). Once again, it is tempting to draw a parallel between Grahame (who made frequent trips to the southern Europe, "the warm South") and Rat's indecision, especially as the narrator places himself firmly with the "stay-at-homes." In the extended metaphor with which the chapter opens, of "Nature's Grand Hotel" the "boarders" watch visitors leave, "and *we miss them, and feel resentful*" (155; emphasis added).

Certainly, this slow-paced chapter, which echoes at its beginning Mole's first walk among the Rabbits, is very seductively written. "The great ring of Downs" which previously shut out the undesirable Wide World now hems him in; "On this side of the hills was now the real blank" (161).

It is almost as if, now that the Mole has given up the attempt at flight, and has failed his creator, so the "admirable" Rat might take up the challenge. And Grahame makes it very clear what is at stake: "With closed eyes he dared to dream a moment in full abandonment, and when he looked again the river seemed steely and chill, the green fields grey and lightless. Then his loyal heart seemed to cry out on his weaker self for its treachery" (160).

The Sea Rat's siren voice does more than merely tempt him: it changes the Water Rat altogether—and Grahame, in a curious treachery of his own, does not grant Rat free will. When Mole meets him, dressed for travel, at the very instant that he "stepped across the threshold" he sees "not his friend's eyes, but the eyes of some other animal!" (174).

And now it is Mole's turn to repress, to be the pupil who has learned his lesson all too well. Ironically, perhaps he begins the "cure" by becoming "lyrical" about the riverbank and "the hearty joys of its snug home life" (176)—as Carpenter points out, this is the Mole who, as we saw in chapter 2, was "no poet himself and didn't care who knew it" (23).[27] The circle is complete, and poetry, the static, the comfortable—and the ultimately inactive—provides the cure for this madness. Indeed, it has been argued that Mole is now wiser than his mentor. Exploring the echoes of the romantic poets in *The Wind in the Willows*, Lesley Willis suggests that "Sadness there certainly is after Ratty's encounter with the Seafarer—the sense of a once-in-a-lifetime opportunity missed—but such wisdom as accrues to Ratty derives not from the Seafarer but from Mole," for Mole has been close to death (in the Wild Wood) and has learned the lesson of conservatism.[28] Rat exercises the same influence (albeit as the lieutenant of Badger) on Toad when he comes home, appealing to common codes of behavior and decency: "'Now, stop swaggering and arguing, and be off! I'll have something to say to you later!'" (200). The effect of the chapter "'Like Summer Tempests Came His Tears,'" apart from being a quiet coda to Toad's adventures, is to reestablish the world of the riverbank vis-à-vis the "human" world, and Rat as its primary citizen.

Toward the end of the book, though, Rat is absorbed into the common group. It may be he who finally lays the law down to Toad ("Try and grasp the fact that on this occasion we're not arguing with you; we're just telling you" [235]) but he is stating the corporate view: he is part of the resolved, conservative stability to which *The Wind in the Willows* points.

The Rat is also the prime mover, as poet perhaps, in the most questionable episode in the book, "The Piper at the Gates of Dawn." In a sense, it is another kind of initiation for Mole, but it is an essential part of life for Rat:

> "O Mole! the beauty of it! The merry bubble and joy, the thin, clear, happy call of the distant piping! Such music I never dreamed of, and the call in it is stronger even than the music is sweet! Row on, Mole, row! For the music and the call must be for us."
>
> The Mole, greatly wondering, obeyed. "I hear nothing myself," he said, "but the wind playing in the reeds and rushes and osiers." (124)

This episode, whose language we shall consider later, has been regarded by some critics as "an error of judgement on a grand scale." Carpenter feels that "Pan does not seem to be the right figure to stand for the pure artistic inspiration, the experience of real poetry," and we should remember that Rat is the essential intermediary in this poetic-mystic process.[29] As a pivotal character, the embodiment of a mode of life, the Rat is in some ways an unsatisfactory figure, for he holds within him, as it were, the seeds of dissatisfaction with the very ideal that the book seems to pursue. (It could also be argued that Mole—and perhaps Grahame—unconsciously came to see that Rat is not the ideal person that he—or they—first thought him to be.) He is also, of course, only Mole's first mentor, and certainly does not represent the father figure of his second, Mr. Badger. Badger stands above Rat—and indeed above most of the characters; but, again, it is virtually impossible to find agreement on just what he is.

THE KINDLY BADGER

> It was the Badger, who . . . had turned round in his chair and was looking at them severely. When he saw that he had secured their attention, and that they were evidently waiting for him to address them, he turned back to the table again and reached out for the cheese. (213)

Badger has made a great impression on the readers of *The Wind in the Willows*. C. S. Lewis, for example, singled him out in his "On

Three Ways of Writing for Children": "Consider Mr Badger in *The Wind in the Willows*,—that extraordinary amalgam of high rank, coarse manners, gruffness, shyness, and goodness. The child who has once met Mr Badger has ever afterwards in its bones a knowledge of humanity and of English social history which it could not get in any other way."[30]

The critics seem to be agreed that Badger is of "high rank"—but what does that mean? Carpenter is in no doubt: "Badger is, of course, a member of the old aristocracy . . . his vast tunnelled dwelling—the great country house and its estate dominating the villagers." This could be argued with on several counts—most notably that Badger is a recluse. Robson is a little less precise: "He exercises natural authority. He is an aristocrat."[31] This, interestingly, contrasts with an American view of him (very much from outside the British class system): "Badger's class is less certain . . . to some he seems close to an older breed of country squiredom, whose potential for antisocial gruffness and boasting ignorance, or, alternatively, benevolent naivety was immortalized by Fielding in the figures of Squire Western and Squire Allworthy. To others he seems more like an old family retainer."[32]

I am inclined to sympathize with the idea that there is something of the squire about Badger, but the emphasis is generally on his age and lineage rather than his precise rank. As he tells Mole: "There were badgers here, I've been told, long before that same city ever came to be. And now there are badgers here again. We are an enduring lot, and we may move out for a time, but we wait, and are patient, and back we come. And so it will ever be" (73).

Other critics have been inclined to emphasize these archetypal characteristics: for example, Fred Inglis describes him as "older, larger, wiser, more shaggy and authoritative, as Senior Clubman/commanding officer/judge/ideal father. Badger is untidy and shabby and crustily careless of manners and correctness; his morality is that of good form and a decent gentlemanliness." Margaret Blount, on the other hand, calls him "lordly, ill-mannered."[33]

The important phrase is, I think, Inglis's, particularly "ideal father." The Badger is stern and practical, yet sympathetic as well; he controls the fearsome wood of nightmares, he is custodian of the warm kitchen. He is "common" and doesn't worry about manners, and yet knows what is the "rule" even in the most outlandish social circumstances; one would not be at all surprised were he spontaneously to set forth rules for "what to do when you have just recaptured your house." It seems fitting that he should have a lot in common with the Mole, and that the book should end not merely with him but with an emphasis on his feeling for children:

> But when the infants were fractious and quite beyond control, they [the mother weasels] would quiet them by telling how, if they didn't hush them and not fret them, the terrible grey Badger would up and get them. This was a base libel on Badger, who, though he cared little about Society, was rather fond of children. . . . (241)

Initially, then, Badger appears as the superior father figure, who rather pointedly puts Rat in his place—in fact, Rat is already diminished by having had to ask for help:

> "O, Badger," cried the Rat, "let us in, please. It's me, Rat, and my friend Mole, and we've lost our way in the snow."
> "What, Ratty, my dear little man!" exclaimed the Badger, in quite a different voice. "Come along in, both of you, at once. Why, you must be perished. . . ." He looked kindly down on them and patted both their heads. "This is not the sort of night for small animals to be out," he said paternally. "I'm afraid you've been up to some of your pranks again, Ratty." (64)

The Badger, then, is seen as kindly (the word is applied to him three times in chapter 4—and "kind-hearted" once) but very powerful. His adoption of Mole, while explicable in animal terms (both live underground) can also be seen in sociological terms, the rather romantic conception of an underlying connection between the ruling classes and the working classes: both are the salt of the earth. But it is also very tempting to regard Badger as the father figure for which the child/Mole/Grahame is searching, for Grahame was deprived of his own father in childhood.

In the search for Grahame's literary antecedents, Richard Jefferies, the nineteenth century's leading nature writer has been suggested—a suggestion that at first sight seems to be about as inappropriate as *The Times*' reviewer's remark about the "negligible" contribution that *The Wind in the Willows* made to natural history. Jefferies, on the other hand, made a vast contribution to natural history writing; his nature mysticism, though essentially unfocused, was a long way from Grahame's rather overblown quasi-paganism. It is unlikely that Grahame was unaware of Jefferies's books, for the former's essays, especially in *Pagan Papers*, echo them, as we shall see. Equally, it could well be that some of Badger's characteristics were inspired by Jefferies's Alexander Iden (Amaryllis's father) in *Amaryllis at the Fair* (1886). Here is Jefferies's description:

> And Amaryllis, noting how handsome her father's intellectual face looked . . . marvelled how he could be so rough sometimes, and why he talked like the labourers, and wore a ragged coat—he who was so full of wisdom in his other moods, and spoke, and thought, and indeed acted as a perfect gentleman.[34]

This mixture, in a character who crosses divisions of class, power, and race, is one that speaks to readers in general, and also, perhaps, spoke more inwardly to Kenneth Grahame.

THE GREAT MR. TOAD!

> "Such a good fellow, too," remarked the Otter reflectively: "But no stability—especially in a boat!" . . .
> "He is indeed the best of animals," replied Rat. "So simple, so good-natured, and so affectionate. Perhaps he's not very clever—we can't all be geniuses; and it may be that he is both boastful and conceited. But he has got some great qualities, has Toady." (14, 24)

If Badger represents security, the character who dominates the remainder of the book represents anarchy.

Toad, "short and fat" as Milne saw him, was perhaps an amalgam of the infamous (and vulgarly ostentatious) politician and businessman Horatio Bottomley, who was jailed for fraud, and (as Peter Green has suggested) of Oscar Wilde. However, Green's suggestion that this portrait might be an attempt by Grahame to expiate Wilde's death received a firm riposte by a reviewer of his book, Georgina Battiscombe: "One wonders which of the two, Mr Toad or Mr Wilde, would be the more affronted by this suggestion."[35]

Both Toad's role and his class have given rise to a good deal of critical speculation. One of the most attractive ideas is Nicholas Tucker's, that Toad is "a worthy successor and at times a conscious imitation of Shakespeare's Falstaff."[36] Elaborating, Tucker writes that, like Falstaff, "Toad alone has an eye for the women and takes it for granted that the Gaoler's daughter has fallen in love with him, in spite of the social gulf that also separates Falstaff from Doll Tearsheet. Toad's version of his escape from prison improves with each telling very much like Falstaff's Gadshill exploits."[37]

Other assessments are less charitable. Margaret Blount thinks that he is the "manic-depressive Toad"; Inglis sees him as "public schoolboy-playboy-country-house owner"; Tucker and Robson both see him as a spoiled, naughty child.[38] His character may, indeed, have been based in part upon his son, Alastair, who was far from being the angel that his mother painted him to be—or, equally, he may have been another of Grahame's alter egos, a warning as well as a celebration.

His social status is also ambiguous, and again the difference between British and non-British assessments is striking. While Sarah Gilead, writing from Israel, can see him simply as a "squire,"[39] Christopher Clausen (who, at the time of writing his article taught at Virginia Polytechnic Institute), called him "an Edwardian Landed Gentleman."[40] On the other hand, an Englishman with a much closer view of English society is more skeptical: "His exact social position is never made clear . . . it is clear that Toad Hall has been in his family for more than one generation; yet the narrative constantly gives the impression that he is a *parvenu* whose family has bought its way into the squirearchy rather than inherited its position."[41]

There have been some extravagant interpretations of what is perhaps essentially a character of farce. Peter Green, persuasively, saw him as paralleling Odysseus (another link, perhaps, with Jefferies, for the *Odyssey* is the favorite reading of Jefferies's most famous character, Bevis):

> In *The Wind in the Willows* [the] Homeric motif is developed. . . . Most of Toad's adventures bear a certain ludicrous resemblance to Ulysses' exploits in the *Odyssey*; and the resemblance becomes detailed and explicit in the last chapter, which parodies the hero's return and the slaying of the suitor. (Its very title—"The Return of Ulysses"—offers the broadest hints as to what Grahame had in mind.)[42]

Sarah Gilead's further analysis might seem questionable at first. She felt that "The weasels and stoats who have taken over Toad Hall are metaphors for Toad's libidinal aggressive/erotic drives. To rout the unsocialized creatures, Toad must traverse an underground passage (his own dark self) and do battle wielding 'enormous cudgels'"[43] Nevertheless, once we admit biographical parallels, this is as legitimate as any other. What can be said is that Toad is far from being the innocent, light hearted creature of childhood he is sometimes assumed to be.

Toad's most important role in the book is his crossing, as we have seen, from one world to another. Margery Fisher suggests, "The caricaturing of Toad is unique in the book . . . whereas the rest of the characters are men in a men's world."[44] Or rather, animals in an animal's world, for Toad is the character who most often encounters the Wide World: it is he who drives a car, rides a horse, acts as a fireman [stoker] on a train, and negotiates with various humans. Again, commentators are divided over how well Grahame depicts this; perhaps Jay Williams put it best when he wrote, "Technically, the balance between their real and unreal aspects is maintained so well that it is beautiful to contemplate."[45]

When we first encounter Toad, he is at once the irresponsible child, who is boastful and has a short attention span, and yet he is also the sly man of the world who "proceeded to play upon the inexperienced Mole as on a harp" (29). When Badger, Rat, and Mole take Toad in hand, he is by turns a stout eccentric or a giggling schoolboy; some critics have pondered the psychological, not to say sexual, significance of his car made of chairs, and of the crash. These scenes at Toad Hall demonstrate the helplessness of the adult world in the face of the rebel.

By the time Toad is in gaol, he is firmly portrayed as a country gentleman, at least in his own mind—even though he "wailed, and kicked his legs, and refused to be comforted" (135–36). However, once the hot buttered toast has done its work, he is able to describe Toad Hall as "an eligible self-contained gentleman's residence, very unique; dating in part from the fourteenth century, but replete with every modern convenience" (138). He also, with regard to the gaoler's daughter, "could not help half-regretting that the social gulf between them was so very wide" (139). There is a certain uneasy comedy generated from the gap between how Toad sees himself and how the gaoler's daughter sees him, and how the line between the animal and human world is examined perhaps a little too closely for comfort. Despite the force of Toad's personality, it is at points like this that the fabric of *The Wind in the Willows* is in danger of coming apart:

> Then she wanted to know about his animal-friends, and was very interested in all he had to tell her about them and how they lived, and what they did to pass their time. Of course, she did not say she was fond of animals as *pets*, because she had the sense to see that Toad would be extremely offended. (138)

Toad, then, is presented as at least two quite different characters simultaneously, whereas the duality in Badger, Mole, and Rat only reveals itself occasionally. Toad is a landowner with a "fine old manner—a blend of the Squire and the College Don" (145); he is also a comic buffoon of farce, a wild child, and, occasionally, a toad.

Consider him, dressed as a washerwoman, attempting to buy a ticket at a train station. To begin with, there is no doubt as to his humanity: by the end of the paragraph, Grahame has related him to the animal kingdom—but so strong is the image of Toad as human, that now the "animals" or "productions" to which the narrator/Toad's consciousness so sardonically refers become mere metaphors for humans. (I shall consider the linguistic trickery at work here in chapter seven.)

> He gave the name of the station that he knew to be nearest to the village of which Toad Hall was the principal feature, and mechanically put his fingers, in search of the necessary money, where his waistcoat pocket should have been. But here the cotton gown . . . intervened, and frustrated his efforts. . . . At last—somehow—he never rightly understood how—he burst the barriers, attained the goal, arrived at where all waistcoat pockets are eternally situated, and found—not only no money, but no pocket to hold it, and no waistcoat to hold the pocket!
>
> To his horror he recollected that he had left both coat and waistcoat behind him in his cell, and with them his pocket-book, money, keys, watch, matches, pencil-case—all that makes life worth living, all that distinguishes the many-pocketed animal, the lord of creation, from the inferior one-pocketed or no-pocketed productions that hop or trip about permissively, unequipped for the real contest. (145)

Confronted with the problem of how to get Toad onto a train, Grahame said, disarmingly, that "the Toad was train-sized and the train was Toad-sized, and therefore there could be no illustrations." Certainly there are a very few scenes that are unillustratable, but that is not a matter of size—Toad is, after all, flexible enough to be able to ride a horse and to feed a furnace. It is at the points where the change of size takes place, where *The Wind in the Willows* is "unstable," that the effects of the book become purely verbal. In this respect, Toad's encounter with the barge-woman is the key scene in the book. In it Toad is again the country gentleman, swelled with pride (like a toad, perhaps), yet it is his *name* that produces the incongruity. The barge-woman—and for only the second instance in the book—equates his name, which he proclaimed so proudly, with the animal, in an association has been totally forgotten by virtually every reader; but this denigration is immediately defused by the fact that his "crawly" toadness was *not* immediately obvious to her. This is a virtuoso piece of writing, and it is rather difficult to support the argument that it demonstrates that Grahame never actually resolved the relationships between his characters and the human world.

> Toad's temper, which had been simmering viciously for some time, now fairly boiled over, and he lost all control of himself.
> "You common, low, *fat* barge-woman!" he shouted; "don't you dare to talk to your betters like that! Washerwoman indeed! I would have you know that I am a Toad, a very well-known, respected, distinguished Toad! I may be under a bit of a cloud at present, but I will *not* be laughed at by a barge-woman!"
> The woman moved nearer to him and peered under his bonnet keenly and closely. "Why, so you are!" she cried. "Well, I never! A horrid, nasty, crawly Toad! And in my nice clean barge, too! Now that is a thing that I will *not* have." (183)

Even when Grahame describes her as unceremoniously throwing him off the barge (by his "hind-legs" and "fore-legs") he makes no effort to reconcile the true woman-toad scale: Toad is now something of the size that he appears in the Shepard drawings— half-human.

The final two chapters, as has been implied, are the most stable, and, at least from a technical point of view, the simplest in the book. Toad is reabsorbed, via the Rat, into society; he has returned to his own world, where he is Toad of Toad Hall, and there is no ambiguity about size. Indeed, his character rapidly shifts away from its child aspect to its irresponsible-adult aspect: he becomes, to all intents and purposes, human. (This defuses Beatrix Potters's famous objection to the scene in the last chapter, when Toad is getting ready for his modest entrance: "Yes—Kenneth Grahame ought to have been an artist— at least all writers for children ought to have a sufficient recognition of what things look like—did he not describe "Toad" as combing his *hair?* A mistake to fly in the face of nature—A frog may wear galoshes; but I don't hold with toads having beards or wigs! so I prefer Badger.[46])

As a human, he must take his place in society. As Badger puts it, in a speech that pretends to be objective but is in fact riddled with repressive class prejudice: "This good fellow has got to live here, and hold his own, and be respected. Would you have him a common laughing-stock, mocked and jeered at by stoats and weasels?" (236).

And so, Toad straddles the two major sections of the book, and the animal and human worlds; he speaks to both farce and a kind of tragedy, and to the child and to the frustrated adult rebel. The result is that his actions raise questions about the wider symbolism that exists in *The Wind in the Willows*.

6

Undercurrents and Whirlpools: Political and Universal Themes

There was nothing to alarm him at first entry. Twigs crackled under his feet, logs tripped him, funguses on stumps resembled caricatures, and startled him for the moment by their likeness to something familiar and far away; but that was all fun, and exciting. (44)

"No Problems"

"Now, you look out, Rat! When Toad's quiet and submissive, and playing at being the hero of a Sunday-school prize, then he's at his artfullest. There's sure to be something up." (106–07)

Kenneth Grahame made two statements about *The Wind in the Willows* which are, as it were, hostages to fortune. The first, already noted, appears in the letter of 10 October 1908 to Theodore Roosevelt which accompanied a copy of *The Wind in the Willows*: "Its qualities, if any, are mostly negative—i.e.—no problems, no sex, no second meaning. . . ." Peter Green, Grahame's biographer and most distinguished critic, was moved, perhaps not surprisingly, to observe that "this is so flagrantly untrue that one's curiosity is at once aroused."[1] We have seen that the characters of the book can be read on many levels; but is this true of the rest of the book as well? We have concentrated on what the characters might mean, largely in relation to the inner life of the author—but what of the wider world? What outward-looking themes and symbols are there? Where does the book's apparently universal appeal lie? And what, in modern critical parlance, are the text's "blindnesses"—after all, what the book does not say is just as striking as what it *does* say.

The Wind in the Willows obviously cannot be as innocent as Grahame claimed—indeed, why should a man with such keen literary knowledge pretend (or believe) that it was? The claim, in fact, clearly encapsulates an idealistic wish for, or about, the book, just as the whole book may be seen as an arcadia, a retreat.

The second pertinent statement is the note that Grahame wrote in July 1908, when he was asked by the publisher, Methuen, for a "descriptive paragraph" to introduce his book:

> I will jot down on the fly-leaf of this some material for a descriptive paragraph for the announcement list, though probably anyone else would do it be better.
>
> 'A book of Youth—and so perhaps chiefly *for* Youth, and those who still keep the spirit of youth alive in them: of life, sunshine, running water, woodlands, dusty roads, winter firesides; free of problems, clean of the clash of sex; of life as it might fairly be supposed to be regarded by some of the wise small things
>
> "That glide in grasses and rubble of woody wreck."'[2]

It may well seem that literary critics devote a good deal of time inventing rather than discovering second meanings (although, given the fundamental role that the reader undeniably plays in *making* meaning, this is assertion not as presumptuous as it may seem at first).

However, if many texts of lasting influence and success derive a good deal of their interest from the ways and extents to which they allow ideas to resonate, then *The Wind in the Willows* is surely such a text; in this respect, it is useful to look more closely at the points made in the Roosevelt letter.

First, negativity: Grahame seems to have meant that disturbing elements are *absent* from his book. However, what we have seen by examining the characters is the negative approach to life in general which lurks beneath the generally sunny surface. *The Wind in the Willows* deals with the "normalization" of Mole and Toad, two disturbing elements, into the world of the status quo. At the end of the book, it is not peace that is restored but the *lack of progress*: throughout, despite rebellious twitches from the young (or young in heart) as represented by Mole and Toad, the deeply conservative figures of Rat and Badger dominate.

> Sometimes, in the course of long summer evenings, the friends would stroll together in the Wild Wood, *now successfully tamed so far as they were concerned*, and it was pleasing to see how respectfully they were greeted by the inhabitants. . . . (241; emphasis added)

In short, the ruling order has been restored: the lower middle classes represented by Mole have been absorbed, the nouveau-riche perhaps represented by Toad have been brought into line, the working classes of the Wild Wood have been put back in their place. Arcadia is safe again—indeed, it might even have expanded: Rat no longer needs his weapons or incantations for a stroll with his friends in the Wild Wood. But just as we might suspect that the Wild Wood, although subdued, may not actually welcome its conquerors, we might also suspect that Grahame's arcadia is built on a series of denials and evasions. The world that he describes so lovingly and lyrically is the masculine world in which he and his friends tramped around during weekends. We can see his world very clearly in *The Wind in the Willows*, but it can also be found in his earlier writings, for example, "Loafing," written for the *National Observer* in January 1891:

But in the South perhaps the happiest loafing-ground is the gift of
Father Thames. . . . I know one little village in the upper reaches
where . . . the early hours of the morning are vexed by the voice of
boaters making their way down the little street to the river. . . . All
this the Loafer hears through the open door of his cottage, where
in his shirt-sleeves he is dallying with his bacon, as a gentleman
should. . . . The Loafer quits the village; and now the world is
before him. Shall he sit on a gate and smoke? or lie on the grass
and smoke? or smoke aimlessly and at large along the road?

The Loafer has a choice: one choice is to lie on his back on the
"breezy downs." The passage that follows—"gazing up into the sky,
his fleshy integument seems to drop away, and the spirit ranges at will
among the tranquil clouds. This way Nirvana nearest lies. . . ."—is
extremely close to the nature-mysticism of Richard Jefferies, especially in *The Story of My Heart* (1884). But Grahame is basically made of
solider stuff, and he comes back to earth for beer ("beer is a thing of
deity—beer is divine"), and to mock at the lunatic boaters, the hoi
polloi.[3]

Now, it hardly needs saying that such an attitude can only subsist
on privilege, and privilege can only be supported by certain kinds of
evasion. But even Grahame was unable to keep his fears, and perhaps
the fears of his generation, out of the book.

THE THREAT ON THE HORIZON

"Animals took sides, as always happens. The River-bankers stood up
for you . . . but the Wild Wood animals said hard things. . . . And
they got very cocky. . . ."
"That's the sort of little beasts they are." (203–4)

As we have seen in briefly examining the historical background,
Grahame's life spanned one of the most turbulent periods of English
history: the social and political order was changing, the countryside

was changing, and male hegemony was being challenged. Grahame and his literary friends looked back to a rural, aristocratic idyll (conveniently ignoring the realities of rural life that Hardy, for example, saw) or looked away to myth, ignoring (unlike Kipling) the toughness of the native characters of folklore.

But looking away does not dispel fear, and fear appears on the horizon in the first few pages of *The Wind in the Willows*:

> "What lies over *there?*" asked the Mole, waving a paw towards a background of woodland that darkly framed the water-meadows on one side of the river.
> "That? O, that's just the Wild Wood," said the Rat shortly. "We don't go there very much, we river-bankers." (9)

The population of the Wild Wood is clearly the new order of the unsettled and unsettling workers, the stoats and weasels, undifferentiated by the uppercasing that the novel's other animal characters merit, and ineffectual rabbits (so ineffectual, indeed, that their distant relatives are included in the gipsy's stew). As Rat says, unconvincingly, "They're all right in a way—I'm very good friends with them—pass the time of day when we meet and all that—but they break out sometimes" (10)—out of the ghetto, presumably.

The only thing that can stand against the "little evil wedge-shaped" faces, with "hard" eyes is the natural authority of Badger, and the superior firepower, in terms of teeth, of Otter, or the pistols and cudgel of Rat. The attitude of the riverbankers to the Wild Wooders is similar to that which the law-givers and law-keepers of the jungle have to the monkeys in Kipling's *The Jungle Book* (1894). In Rat's terms, you need to be an expert—you need to be initiated, streetwise, to survive:

> Besides, there are a hundred things one has to know, which we understand all about, and you don't as yet. I mean passwords, and signs, and sayings which have power and effect, and plants you carry in your pocket, and verses you repeat, and dodges and tricks you practise; all simple enough when you know them, but they've got to be known if you're small, or you'll find yourself in trouble. (49)

One of Kipling's recurrent themes was that of the "inner circle," and Rat's lesson to Mole resembles the lessons of Baloo to Mowgli (and Baloo, it should be remembered, is the exact opposite of the genial—if jungle-wise—oaf portrayed by the Disney film): "so Baloo, the Teacher of the Law, taught him the Wood and Water Laws: how to tell a rotten branch from a sound one; how to speak politely to the wild bees . . . how to warn the water-snakes in the pools before he splashed down among them." And, of course, the one thing that Mowgli is warned against particularly is the Bandar-log, the monkey folk:

> They have no law. They are outcasts. . . . They are very many, evil, dirty, shameless, and they desire, if they have any fixed desire, to be noticed by the Jungle-People. But we do *not* notice them even when they throw nuts and filth on our heads.[4]

Such are the lawless of the Wild Wood, too, who abuse the established middle classes, Badger and Mole, and drop a rock onto Toad, who (symbolically?) is in Rat's boat and clothing at the time. When they take over Toad Hall, they lie in bed and eat breakfast at all hours—precisely as Toad does, and the parallel degeneracy is clear—and they are rather disorganized and inclined to fight among themselves. And, of course, their moral code is so slack that they cheat by having firearms, a course that Rat (who knows his enemies' habits) is inclined to emulate, but which Badger will have none of. Toad Hall is regained, most improbably, by basic, manly means: just as in the popular literature of Grahame's childhood one Englishman was worth ten foreigners, so the Englishman would fight with his fists, not with weapons. (In *The Flying Inn* (1914) and in his "Father Brown" stories, G. K. Chesterton makes great play of the straightness of the Englishman's sword as against the scimitars of the heathen.) As the Badger says, when the Rat loads him down with weapons: "All right, Ratty! It amuses you and it doesn't hurt me. I'm going to do all I've got to do with this here stick" (223). And once they have cleared Toad Hall of the vulgar masses, they retire to bed, "safe in Toad's ancestral home, won back by matchless valour, consummate strategy, and a proper handling of sticks" (231). This distinction between proper and improper ways of fighting has, after all, survived into film: how often in a Western or a thriller does the villain take up some illegitimate weapon?

Of course, the four heroes have another, much subtler weapon—history. The secret passage under Toad Hall, like Badger's passages under the Wild Wood, are ancestral: they predate and are superior to anything that the rising workers can accomplish. The stoats and weasels are also divided among themselves, whereas the natural rulers are united. Toad's worst crime lies not in breaking the law but in breaking ranks. As the Rat says, "When are you going to be sensible, and think of your friends, and try and be a credit to them? Do you suppose it's any pleasure for me, for instance, to hear animals saying, as I go about, that I'm the chap that keeps company with gaol-birds?" (201).

The "civil war" is the visible face of an enemy, but they present as well an *invisible* aspect: where, after all, are the servants at Toad Hall, Rat's house, or even at "Mole End"? This kind of "absence" is not necessarily political. Robert Leeson, in his polemical history of children's books, *Reading and Righting* has pointed out that the "uninhibited" middle-class children of books by Frances Hodgson Burnett or Edith Nesbit, are supported by "the anonymous figure of the servant. . . . In the 1890s and early 1900s, while the 'free' child is wrecking the nursery and roaming the woods, half a million anonymous children went hungry to school."[5] There was a deliberate, if unconscious, marginalising of the lower classes.

These "absences" also occur in *The Wind in the Willows*, although they may, perhaps charitably, be accounted for in purely technical ways. In 1919 a Professor G. T. Hill inquired as to who had maintained "Mole End" between Mole's sudden departure and his return. Grahame replied that the questions "are probably best answered by a simple reference to the hopelessly careless and slipshod methods of the author," while suggesting that that Mole could have afforded a char-mouse. He goes on:

> In support of his theory, I would ask you to observe that our author practises a sort of "character economy" which has the

81

appearance of being deliberate. The presence of certain characters may be indicated in or required by the story, but if the author has no immediate use for them, he simply ignores their existence. Take this very question of domestic service—however narrow poor Mole's means may have been, it is evident that Rat was comfortably off—indeed I strongly suspect him of a butler-valet and cook-housekeeper. Toad Hall, again, must have been simply crawling with idle servants eating their heads off.

But the author doesn't happen to want them, so for him they simply don't exist. He doesn't say they are *not* there: he just leaves them alone.[6]

The example that Grahame gives, of the absence of a stoker on the train aboard which Toad escapes, is perhaps the extreme example of this—while the Badger, who seems to lead a solitary existence is able to "send someone" to take the little hedgehogs home through the snow. We are told at the end of chapter 2 that Toad has a housekeeper, and food appears at key intervals at Rat's house. Perhaps Grahame is right that such things need not be accounted for, otherwise we are led into wondering what the stoats and weasels did with the servants when they took over . . . or, perhaps, what happened to Lady Macbeth's children!

But the denial of the class that supports the luxurious lives of the riverbankers runs a great deal deeper than purely technical convenience, and there has been a brilliant exposition of the subtext of class in Jan Needle's novel *Wild Wood*, which is *The Wind in the Willows* retold from the point of view of the stoats and the weasels.

It is an ingenious piece: the Sea Rat and the gaoler's daughter, even the drivers of the car that Toad hijacks at the end are all part of the same plot. The characters are named after independent British brewers of "real ale": the narrator is a downtrodden ferret called Baxter. Baxter, who works at the local garage, is very much a victim of the class system; trying to support his "mother and six brothers and sisters," he loses his job when Toad crashes the car he has stolen (65). He then loses his *next* job when he tries to deliver a new car to Toad Hall. This is a particularly clever and telling interweaving of the old book and the new. In *The Wind in the Willows* the scene is played as comedy—aristocratic comedy, at that:

> The Badger strode up the steps. "Take him inside," he said stern-ly to his companions. Then, as Toad was hustled through the door, struggling and protesting, he turned to the chauffeur in charge of the new motor-car.
>
> "I'm afraid you won't be wanted to-day," he said. "Mr. Toad has changed his mind. He will not require the car. Please under-stand that this is final. You needn't wait." Then he followed the others inside and shut the door. (100–101)

In Needle's version, on the other hand, the downtrodden Baxter is still sitting in the car:

> The row in the hallway was something shocking. I tried to speak to the badger, tried to argue, like. But it was no good. He turned on his heel and disappeared, slamming the door behind him.
>
> So there I sat—jobless once more. . . . I was fed up with all this. . . . Fed up with never knowing when my next wage packet might be snatched from me without so much as a by-your-leave.[7]

It might be observed that Shepard, with his illustration, colludes with Grahame here: it presents the automobile, but does not show the driver's seat. But perhaps the most telling message of *Wild Wood* is that however much the middle and upper classes, in their arrogance and ignorance, are manipulated and supported by the working classes, they will nevertheless win because the cards of wealth and power are firmly stacked against the working classes. Ironically, this is precisely the same message that Grahame gives in *The Wind in the Willows*—dif-fering only in that Needle disapproves of the situation of which Grahame approves.

Thus, in *The Wind in the Willows* the world is made safe by com-edy (just as we shall see in the next chapter that it is made safe by lan-guage). When the ferret sentry raises his rifle, "Toad prudently dropped flat in the road, and *Bang!* a bullet whistled over his head"

(222). When the young stoats drop a stone into the boat in which Toad is rowing, "with great glee" they call out "It'll be your head next time, Toady!" (209). The triumphant recapture of Toad Hall is bloodless and complete, veering from the serious military operation into a slapstick farce. Indeed, the reestablishment of middle-class superiority verges on the callous: Badger, "his mouth full of chicken and trifle," starts to reorganize things by saying, "Mole . . . I want you to take *those fellows on the floor there* upstairs with you, and have some bedrooms cleaned out . . . and made really comfortable" (230; emphasis added). It also turns out, with some convenient political mythologizing, that it is really a few ringleaders who are to blame. Mole comes back and reports:

> They were very penitent, and said they were extremely sorry for what they had done, but it was all the fault of the Chief Weasel and the stoats, and if they could ever do anything for us at any time to make up, we had only got to mention it. (231)

Perhaps the depths of Grahame's wish-fulfillment are reached here. Not only can *The Wind in the Willows* be seen as Grahame's attempt to sublimate his frustrated wish for a father but it also tames the evil world that threatens even his arcadia.

But this is not the only threat: a more insidious one, that crosses class boundaries, comes from *females*.

"CLEAN OF THE CLASH OF SEX"

"But you know what *girls* are, ma'am! Nasty little hussies, that's what *I* call 'em!" (180)

It is by now a truism that the criticism of literature, even the definition of literature itself, has been male-dominated; the female element in books has become all but invisible. One need not be a feminist to observe that questions of sex and gender in *The Wind in the Willows* do not go away simply because they seem not to be mentioned. When Mary Haynes asked schoolchildren in England for their opinion of the book, one schoolgirl wrote: "I did not really think of the characters as animals. I did not notice that they were all males, but now it has been pointed out to me, I am quite annoyed; though somehow females would just not fit into the story."[8]

It is perhaps an impertinent speculation (though biographers have indulged in it) that Grahame, who was a staunch bachelor, could not cope with what is euphemistically described as the "physical side" of his marriage—hence, it might be inferred, the interesting phrase, mentioned above, with which he described the book: "*clean* of the *clash* of sex."

His life seems by all accounts to have been asexual and spent in the society of men. Peter Green mentions, of a friend Grahame met at the Bank of England, that

> Ward recalls an occasion on which Grahame had borrowed a fourteenth-century cottage in the main street of Streatley, and they walked twenty miles along the Ridgeway before returning to "chops, great chunks of cheese, new bread, great swills of beer, pipes, bed, and heavenly sleep."[9]

This is Grahame's own arcadia, and it is hardly surprising that *The Wind in the Willows* is very much *not* about women: when they appear, they are either referred to slightingly or they break the continuity and coherence of the story. As we have seen, of all the characters, the gaoler's daughter and the barge-woman (both deprived of proper names) come closest to shattering the delicate balance of the book: they represent the key points (apart from Rat's solecism about Mole's suit) where the human and animal worlds clash, rather than cohere. While the gypsy, or the car drivers, or the judge, or the people in the railway station, see nothing but a rather buffoonish, short, fat, country gentleman (or washerwoman), the females see an animal. This could scarcely be more degrading for the animals—quite apart from the self-image that human males have by implication. And it also implies misogyny, for the women see the wrong thing: if this is, in a sense, wisdom, it is a wisdom that the male/animal world fears and does not want to acknowledge.

One of the consolations for Toad of being locked into his bedroom by his friends is, as Mole says, "no more weeks in hospital, being ordered about by female nurses" (104). Similarly, the Rat, cataloguing Toad's misadventures with some disdain, points out the depths that he has plumbed:

> "but seriously, don't you see what an awful ass you've been making of yourself? On your own admission you have been handcuffed, imprisoned, starved, chased, terrified out of your life, insulted, jeered at, and ignominiously flung into the water—*by a woman, too!*" (201; emphasis added)

We may be accustomed to male dominance in literature, but *The Wind in the Willows* carries it to a rare extreme. The first actual appearance of a female is, remarkably, on page 135, and it is the gaoler's daughter, a female who derives her very identity from her father's occupation. At this point, Grahame is in the full flight of Toad's adventures, well into the human realm, and well in to the neo-gothic story. And so this female is described in neo-gothic language—a necessary device in this situation. For example, "wench" is a word that not only changes the time perspective, but also the status of the female.

> Now the gaoler had a daughter, a pleasant wench and good-hearted, who assisted her father in the lighter duties of his post. . . . This kind-hearted girl, pitying the misery of Toad, said to her father one day, "Father! I can't bear to see that poor beast so unhappy, and getting so thin! You know how fond of animals I am. I'll make him eat from my hand, and sit up, and do all sorts of things." (135)

As we have seen, there is a subtle blurring in this scene between Toad as gentleman and Toad as toad. The mismatch between what Toad is, on the one hand, and what the gaoler's daughter is, on the other—as well as in how they see each other—suggests that Grahame is, here more than anywhere else in the book, uncomfortable with the situation. He is at once insulting to the female—she "liked that bit [about the linen presses] especially"—and comes close to destroying the animal world ("I'll make him eat out of my hand"). The gaoler's daughter's interest in Toad's "animal-friends" might just be equated with a working girl's interest in the aristocracy—but it reads rather more like Alice looking down on the creatures in the pool of tears: they are seen as mere whimsies. That Grahame is on very dangerous ground is shown by Toad's "half-regretting that the social gulf between them was so very wide, for she was a comely lass, and evidently admired him very much" (139). The element of farce becomes decidedly uncomfortable here, whatever the echoes of the folktale.

On the other hand, the gaoler's daughter is portrayed as kind, gentle—and the provider of the nursery delight of hot buttered toast. In one sense, this "compassionate virgin" image is also oppressive of women, but within it may lie Grahame's fundamental longing for a caring woman in an asexual relationship.

The next female to appear, the girl's aunt, appears, as we shall see, under the artifice of reported, pantomime language (though the joke that introduces her may not be as innocent to women as it may seem to men):

> "Toad," she said presently, "just listen, please. I have an aunt who is a washerwoman."
>
> "There, there," said Toad graciously and affably, "never mind; think no more about it. *I* have several aunts who *ought* to be washerwomen." (139)

And by the time that Toad is humiliated by the barge-woman, the intrusion of women, whether large and fat or young and comely is uncomfortably complete: they are even more threatening than the Wild Wooders. Only when life has been restored to absolute normality, and the riverbankers can stroll in the Wild Wood, do mothers appear.

Such is the urge for male dominance that even the search for the lost little Otter, in "The Piper at the Gates of Dawn," is exclusively male. There must, presumably, be a Mrs. Otter, but she is never seen, and is mentioned only by implication as an adjunct of Otter himself.

Thus, *The Wind in the Willows* is far from being "free of the clash of sex": women are so potent a threat that they are excluded from the book as much as possible. Where they do intrude, they disturb its structure, language, and balance. Even their appearance is powerful: when Toad escapes from the gaol, "The washerwoman's squat figure . . . seemed a passport for every barred door and grim gateway" (142). And what puts the sentries at Toad Hall into disarray? Mole in the very same costume.

It might be argued that these are all manifestations of power, rather than of sexuality, but Grahame seems to come perilously close to symbolism that is highly suggestive. Guided by the (traditionally female) moon, Rat and Mole, in their two-person boat—another suggestive image—approach the most dangerous point on the river:

> In midmost of the stream, embraced in the weir's shimmering arm-spread, a small island lay anchored, fringed close with willow and silver birch and alder. Reserved, shy, but full of significance, it hid whatever it might hold behind a veil, keeping it till the hour should come, and, with the hour, those who were called and chosen. (134)

In using sensual and metaphoric language, Grahame seems to have drifted into very questionable sexual waters.

THE RIVER BANK AND THE OPEN ROAD

"So-this-is-a-River!"
"The River," corrected the Rat. (9)

Flowing, almost literally, through *The Wind in the Willows* is a coherent group of symbols, with the river at its center. Grahame was raised by the River Thames, and returned to live near it for most of his adult life—indeed, he spent his last afternoon by it.[10] This is convenient for symbol hunters, of course, for the river can be taken to connote everything from sexuality to innocence, from comfort to threat. We might reflect on the fact that the only illustration in the first edition of *The Wind in the Willows* was a drawing by W. Graham Robertson of a small waterfall with three naked children, presumably cherubs, beside it. The caption was, "And a River Went Out from Eden" (a line, of course, from the second chapter of the book of Genesis): this is the innocent world, free of sexuality and sin, imminently under threat.

More specifically, it is important that the river in *The Wind in the Willows* is not simply *a* river: it is (although this is not, of course, explicitly stated in the book), the River Thames, "Old Father Thames," the river that is in some ways a symbol of Englishness. It flows through the Oxford that Grahame was denied and on into the Berkshire, through one of the most civilized, secure, and wealthy areas of England. The valley is bounded by the "great ring of Downs" (171), the places where Grahame so often walked, and so the setting of *The Wind in the Willows* has both personal significance for the author and broader cultural significance for the British (especially for the English).

(It is an interesting sidelight to the literary symbolism of *The Wind in the Willows* that the same downs (although a little to the west) later served as the *opposite* symbol in Richard Adams's *Watership*

Down (1972), a phenomenal best-seller in Britain and the United States in the 1970s.

Just as the seasons depicted so lavishly in the book are both real and ideal, so the river valley is both a specific and symbolic setting. When the book came to be illustrated, this presented some problems. E. H. Shepard was able to visit the river, but Grahame was too frail to accompany him.

> I poked and pried along the river bank to find where was Rat's boat-house, and where Mole had crossed the water to join him, and, as I listened to the river noises . . . I could almost fancy that I could see a tiny boat pulled up against the reeds (iv)

Images, of course, can be very successful, but to make the setting too specific, as Shepard does in the map that appears in some editions of *The Wind in the Willows* (called, curiously, "A map of the Wild Wood and Surrounding Country") detracts from the essentially personal, uncommunicable image in the reader's mind.

We have seen that the river forms the center of the battle between retreat and adventure: it is at once Toad's playground and Rat's way of life. If this conflict is a key theme of children's literature, so is the theme of initiation—and the river is again very potent. Rat's phrase—"messing about in boats" (6) has passed into the idiom of British English, and the difference between Mole the outsider and Mole the insider can be seen in his knowledge of boats. Early in chapter 1, "The River Bank," Mole admits that he has never been in a boat in his life: Toad's story begins on the riverbank, where the insiders are at work:

> The Mole and the Water rat had been up since dawn very busy on matters connected with boats and the opening of the boating season; paining and varnishing, mending paddles, repairing cushions, hunting for missing boathooks, and so on. . . . (97)

There is an incantatory element here, the language of the initiated, whom the reader can join vicariously. Among Grahame's predecessors a very similar attitude to craftsmanship—particularly the craft of boats—is found in Richard Jefferies's *Bevis*; among his contemporaries in Rudyard Kipling's *Rewards and Fairies* (1910), notably in the story "The Wrong Thing"; and among his followers in Arthur Ransome's *Swallows and Amazons* and its successors. In the fifth book of the Ransome series, *Coot Club,* the freshwater-sailing children meet a salt-water sailor, who, in a delicious litany

> showed them all kinds of knots and other things that can be made with rope, Bowlines and Fisherman's and Carrick bends, Rolling, Blackwall, Timber and Handspike hitches, Cat's Paws and Sheepshanks, Eye splices and Long splices, Grommets and a Selvagee strop. They had not heard half the names. . . .[11]

Craft, after all, is central to the traditions of conservatism, and boating, of one sort or another, is one of the totems of English life. When the Sea Rat says, "I see by your build that you're a fresh-water mariner," he is acknowledging a profound brotherhood.

The arcadia of the riverbank appeals to a very deep nostalgia for a golden world. It is a nostalgia found in most generations, and this sense of an ideal past was strong in Grahame himself. In celebrating it, he created a mythological past for today's readers. Some indication of the cultural strength of this synthetic past can be found in the way in which, as noted, the advertising industry has used *The Wind in the Willows* to promote a "'real England' of ancient monuments and of small villages virtually untouched by social and economic change . . . the nation's real home."[12] The irony of that advertising campaign is that it showed the characters traveling in a car. As Tony Watkins observes, in *The Wind in the Willows* "modern technology, in the form of the motor car, is presented in a highly ambivalent manner. . . . [It is] the source of noise and terror and danger in the countryside."[13] The automobile has presented a paradox to writers in England: after the World War I there was an epidemic of writers who were smitten with nostalgia, who traveled England *by car* in search, they thought, of the "real" spirit of the place. Most famous of these was probably H. V. Morton, whose *In Search of England* (1927) describes driving into

Stratford-upon-Avon ("full of long-legged girls from America") "through a perfect death-rattle of motor traffic."[14] For Grahame, it marked the beginning of the end.

The connections between humans, mechanical items, and the degradation of a way of life are clear. Rat talks about "steamers that flung hard bottles—at least bottles were certainly flung, and *from* steamers, so presumably *by* them" (22), while the field mice want to move house "before those horrid machines begin clicking round the fields" (156). However, it is the automobile, that "small cloud of dust, with a dark centre of energy, advancing on them at incredible speed"—with its wail (significantly) "like an uneasy animal in pain" (33)—that symbolizes both freedom and destruction throughout the book. Some critics have wondered why Grahame did not include the railway in his general condemnation of "progress," but that is easily explained. John Moore, looking back from the scarred world of 1946 to his arcadian village of Brensham in the 1920s, writes about the charabanc, that is, the early tour bus:

> Now, whereas the impact of charabancs on a village is a defiling thing, for they are devouring monsters which destroy the rural atmosphere without putting anything in its place, the impact of the railway has a very different result. The railway is not sterile like the charabancs; it does not, like them, destroy and then vanish, mosstrooper-fashion, but it remains to become part of the village. . . . Thus Brensham wasn't urbanised by the railway; instead the railway at Brensham was made rural.[15]

To the modern reader, then, this grappling with new technology is a familiar situation, and the freedom of the open road holds the seeds of its destruction: "O what a flowery track lies spread before me, henceforth! What dust-clouds shall spring up behind me as I speed on my reckless way" (36). The primrose path to destruction, in fact—as opposed to the mystic river where the "flowers smiled and nodded from either bank" (130).

FOOD AND KITCHENS

"Oh stop, stop," cried the Mole in ecstasies: "This is too much!"
"Do you really think so?" inquired the Rat seriously. "It's only
what I always take on these little excursions. . . ." (8)

Because *The Wind in the Willows* is a rich store of symbols and
appeals on all kinds of levels, rather than attempting to be exhaustive
I shall consider just two more areas where the interests of child and
adult overlap.

Certain aspects of adult life are not particularly or immediately
relevant to child readers or, it must be said, to the child-in-the-adult
(sexual activity being the most obvious example); these aspects tend to
be addressed in children's literature by replacing them with things that
are relevant to children.

Food is a most obvious choice for such a substitution. Food-
fanciers will find an appetizing journey in store for them in *The Wind
in the Willows*, from Rat's hamper to Toad's banquet. We arrive at the
end of the book via a series of remarkably sensuous evocations—the
unspecified meal at Badger's, the supper at Mole's humble home with
"the lately barren board set thick with savoury comforts" (94), the
bubble-and-squeak (fried leftover potatoes and greens) and buttered
toast that revive Toad in gaol, the amazing gypsy stew, the meals provided by the Rat for the returning Toad at Rat's house, the cold beef
and pickles and cold pie and cheese that Mole and Badger eat there,
and the "guava jelly in a glass dish, and a cold chicken, a tongue . . .
some trifle, and quite a lot of lobster salad" that Mole and Rat assem-
ble for the victors at Toad Hall. It does not take a great deal of analysis
to see that all these meals mark—celebrate—the end of an adventure,
a wholesome, comforting, and satisfying resolution. Where the adventure has been particularly trying there is a *second* meal, to make the
resolution even stronger, as with the the porridge, bacon, fried ham,
and eggs for breakfast at Badger's house, or Toad's meals at Rat's

house. Even the *start* of an adventure requires a "simple but sustaining meal—bacon and broad beans, and a macaroni pudding" (221), while Rat's meal with the Sea Rat has exotic possibilities: "a sausage out of which the garlic sang, some cheese which lay down and cried, and a long-necked straw-covered flask containing bottled sunshine . . ." (169–70). The servants may be invisible, but they lavishly provide a wish-fulfillment that speaks to a very basic part of human nature.

Food, of course, originates in kitchens, and throughout literature the kitchen has come to symbolize the state of the house: if it is stable, then all is well, if it is not, then it is a place of uncertainty and transit. There is no shortage of examples in children's literature: Harriet and the cook are at odds in Louise Fitzhugh's *Harriet the Spy*; Charlotte is not allowed to join in the comfortable life of the kitchen in Edward Ardizzone's *Tim and Charlotte*; and in Edith Nesbit's *The Railway Children*, a kitchen greets the displaced family with "no curtains, no hearth-rug . . . no fire, and the black grate showed cold, dead ashes"[16]—so the first thing the children do the next morning is light the kitchen fire and put the kettle on. Similarly, Humphrey Carpenter cites the cozy kitchen in Kingsley's *The Water-Babies* and the "filth and disorder" of the king's kitchen in MacDonald's *The Princess and Curdie*.[17]

Perhaps the most famous kitchen in children's books (apart from the one that Rat and Mole enter) is that in "Pig and Pepper," chapter 6 of *Alice's Adventures in Wonderland*, a disturbed place in a disturbing book:

> The door led right into a large kitchen, which was full of smoke from one end to the other: the Duchess was sitting on a three-legged stool in the middle, nursing a baby; the cook was leaning over the fire. . . . There was certainly too much [pepper] in the air. Even the Duchess sneezed occasionally; and the baby was sneezing and howling alternately without a moment's pause . . . the cook took the caldron of soup off the fire, and at once set to work throwing everything within her reach at the Duchess and the baby—the fire-irons came first; then followed a shower of saucepans, plates, and dishes.

Undercurrents and Whirlpools: Political and Universal Themes

It is only Alice's calm insouciance that sees her through. Another excellent example of a kitchen that very much sets the tone for the rest of the book is the kitchen in chapter 1 of Emily Brontë's *Wuthering Heights*, where the amount of overexaggeration and distortion sets the tone for the heightened, melodramatic plot that follows. This is a kitchen seen through a convex lens:

> One end . . . reflected splendidly both light and heat from ranks of immense pewter dishes, interspersed with silver jugs and tankards, towering row after row, on a vast oak dresser, to the very roof. . . . Its entire anatomy lay bare . . . except where a frame of wood laden with oatcakes and clusters of legs of beef, mutton, and ham, concealed it. Above the chimney were sundry villainous old guns. . . .

There is no such ambiguity, though, in Badger's kitchen. Here we come to the apotheosis of Grahame's idyll, in perhaps the most quoted part of *The Wind in the Willows*:

> The floor was well-worn red brick, and on the wide hearth burnt a fire of logs, between two attractive chimney-corners tucked away in the wall, well out of any suspicion of draft. A couple of high-backed settles, facing each other on either side of the fire, gave further sitting accommodation for the sociably disposed. . . . Rows of spotless plates winked from the shelves of the dresser at the far end of the room, and from the rafters overhead hung hams, bundles of dried herbs, nets of onions, and baskets of eggs. It seemed a place where heroes could fitly feast after victory, where weary harvesters could line up in scores along the table and keep their Harvest Home with mirth and song, or where two or three friends of simple tastes could sit about as they pleased and eat and smoke and talk in comfort and contentment. The ruddy brick floor smiled up at the smoky ceiling; the oaken settles, shiny with long wear, exchanged cheerful glances with each other; plates on the dresser grinned at the pots on the shelf, and the merry fire-light flickered and played over everything without distinction. (61)

It is a comfortable, comforting scene: a kind of resolution to the rich variety of materials in the book. *The Wind in the Willows* clearly carries many specific and universal resonances, and so our final question might be this: What kind of language can adequately convey such complexity?

7

The Wind in the Reeds—The Eddies of Style

"But what do the words mean?" asked the wondering Mole. (132)

THE LANGUAGE OF CONTRASTS

"I don't know that I think so *very* much of that little song, Rat," observed the Mole cautiously. He was no poet himself and didn't care who knew it; and he had a candid nature. (23)

The ambivalent status of *The Wind in the Willows* does not lie solely in its narrative structure, its characters, and its symbols and themes. Like the errant mayfly Otter disappears in pursuit of, the style of the book swerves unsteadily, even wildly, from paragraph to paragraph and chapter to chapter. Grahame was a very conscious stylist who admired such writers as Sir Thomas Browne, and so it might be assumed that these variations were conscious too. Whether they are or are not, the study of the stylistic variations of *The Wind in the Willows* is in itself a fascinating demonstration of the power of style to shift the way we perceive a text or a situation.

These shifts serve several disparate purposes. What we might call the "instability" of the text means that Grahame can build up his arcadia by lyrical descriptions of the countryside (as in Mole's story), and can extend this into a kind of nature-mysticism in the interpolated chapters; he can use as well another variation to protect this arcadia from intrusions of the real world. He uses style shifts to avoid awkward confrontations—notably in terms of dialogue—to bridge the awkward gaps between fantasy and reality, and to metaphorize the symbols (notably those of sexuality and politics).

Language, then, manipulates the reader, but it also betrays the text's "blindnesses." I have noted, for example, how Grahame's claim that the book is unsullied by sex must be treated with some skepticism, for what it suppressed on the obvious level of the narrative's description resurfaces on a symbolic level; this is also true in terms of the style. Consider the the male-oriented language of Mole's story, where the river is initially seen as "sleek, sinuous, full-bodied animal" (3), or the overblown description of Pan in "The Piper at the Gates of Dawn," or the crescendoes of Toad's motoring ecstasies.

Peter Green has observed that "one factor that tends to be discounted" in the criticism of *The Wind in the Willows* "is the sheer brilliance of Grahame's actual writing." There is no doubt as to its virtuosity. "Good prose, though," Green goes on, has fallen out of fashion these days, and the contemporary reader is more likely to be attracted by Grahame's spare, witty, and often sardonic dialogue."[1] It may well be the juxtaposition of the witty and the "poetic"—two different kinds of sophistication—that helps *The Wind in the Willows* to retain its appeal.

A useful way to examine this juxtaposition of styles is to compare *The Wind in the Willows* with another "Thames" book of the period, with which it has a remarkable affinity, Jerome K. Jerome's *Three Men in a Boat* (1889). Jerome was essentially a humorist, but his book is divided between deadpan slapstick comedy, long stretches of historical romanticism, and turgid quasi-mysticism. As in *The Wind in the Willows*, there is a sense that, beneath the author's flippancy, the river is deeply symbolic, even sexual; the two books hold many other similarities beyond this. There is a preoccupation with food, and parallels to be drawn between the ever-optimistic character of the narrator ("J") and Mole, as well as between the ebullient Harris and Toad; and then there is George, an altogether more bland character, who works in a bank but escapes to the river at weekends. Harris ("what you would call a well-made man of about number one size") has a "fixed idea that he *can* sing a comic song,"[2] quixotically leads people around Hampton Court Maze, and has wild encounters with marauding swans in a way that reminds one inexorably of Toad.

Three Men in a Boat is in many ways the secular apotheosis of the kind of muscular escapism much practiced by Grahame. What is interesting is the way in which exactly the same two styles—the overblown, anthropomorphizing, pseudo-philosophic, and the broad, witty elements of farce—coexist, and how the book's humor makes the mysticism safe.

Jerome is the past master of the anticlimactic: he tends to undercut his "mystical" effects with down-to-earth contrasts. Grahame, on the other hand, does this in rather larger sections—although one feels, perhaps, that some of the more turgid episodes of *The Wind in the Willows* might have benefited from deflation. Here is "J" in *Three Men in a Boat* describing his sailing experiences, which are very reminiscent both of Toad's extravagances and of Rat's mysticism:

> There is no more thrilling sensation I know of than sailing. . . .
> The wings of the rushing wind seem to be bearing you onward,
> you know not where. You are no longer the slow, plodding, puny
> thing of clay, creeping tortuously upon the ground; you are part
> of Nature! Your heart is throbbing against hers. Her glorious arms
> are round you, raising you up against her heart! Your spirit is one
> with hers; your limbs grow light! The voices of the air are singing
> to you. The earth seems far away and little; and the clouds so
> close above your head, are brothers, and you stretch your arms to
> them. . . .

> We seemed like knights of some old legend, sailing across some mystic lake into the unknown realm of twilight, into the great land of the sunset.
>
> We did not go into the realm of twilight; we went slap into that punt. . . .[3]

This technique is also found in another book that has clear affinities to *The Wind in the Willows*, Richard Jefferies's seminal novel *Bevis*. Like *The Golden Age*, *Bevis* is a book that, though it has been adopted *by* children, is very much *about* childhood. One of its features (for it is almost as "unstable" a text as *The Wind in the Willows* in its many effects) is Jefferies's need to keep his nature mysticism in its place, using, like Jerome, the technique of anticlimax. In this extract, Bevis and his friend Mark are sitting with their spaniel, Pan, by a brook:

> The steady roar of the fall, and a rippling sound above it of bursting bubbles and crossing wavelets of the hastening stream, notched and furrowed over stones, frowning in eager haste. The rushing and the coolness, and the song of the brook and the birds, and the sense of the sun sinking, stilled even Bevis and Mark a little while. They sat and listened, and said nothing; the delicious brook filled their ears with music.
>
> The next minute Bevis seized Pan by the neck and pitched him over into the bubbles.[4]

While Grahame balances, for example, the eulogy of summer in "The Wild Wood," chapter 3 of *The Wind in the Willows*, with Mole's experiences in the Wild Wood, there is no such relief in one of the most discussed chapters, "The Piper at the Gates of Dawn." The language of this episode has often been cited as being "too difficult" for children; it is very much of its time, and writers in *The Yellow Book* or impressionable youngsters such as Arthur Ransome, perpetrated similar material. It is, to say the least, unfashionable, and it accompanies, as we have seen, Grahame's explicit drawing of the god, Pan. Grahame creates a perfervid atmosphere:

> Mole stopped rowing as the liquid run of that glad piping broke
> on him like a wave, caught him up, and possessed him utterly. . . .
> For a space they hung there, brushed by the purple loosestrife that
> fringed the bank. . . . On either side of them, as they glided
> onwards, the rich meadow-grass seemed that morning of a fresh-
> ness and a greenness unsurpassable. Never had they noticed the
> roses so vivid, the willow-herb so riotous, the meadow-sweets so
> odorous and pervading. (124–25)

How far the actual description of Pan (Shepard, it might be said, has
the sense to keep the god offstage), with the sensual indulgences in
rippling muscles, broad chest, splendid curves, and shaggy limbs is a
regrettable error of taste is a matter of opinion. What cannot be
denied is the fact that Grahame has used considerable linguistic
resources, which certainly suggests the chapter's importance if not to
subsequent readers then certainly to him. W. W. Robson is emphatic
in his estimation of this chapter: "Historically speaking it was, we
have reason to think, an afterthought on the author's part; artistical-
ly, it is the reason for which the whole book exists."[5] For Neil Philip
the poetic prose and the "pallid Edwardian paganism" are the only
elements of *The Wind in the Willows* with which he is "entirely out of
sympathy," but he pinpoints the immediate influences on Grahame.
The god Pan, originally the god of flocks and shepherds in ancient
Greece, became a fertility symbol and a byword for sudden, apparently motiveless terror (hence "panic"). In "bohemian London," as the
novelist Somerset Maugham put it, "Poets saw him lurking in the twi-
light on London commons, and literary ladies in Surrey, nymphs of
an industrial age, mysteriously surrendered their virginity to his rough
embrace."[6] Philip is scathing about Grahame's treatment: "But it was
his unique achievement to reduce the savage god to a sort of woodland nanny." He goes on:

> Again, a strand of Grahame's neo-paganism derives from
> Stevenson, but how bitterly resonant is Stevenson's sentence in
> the light of Grahame's life and work: "Shrilly sound Pan's pipes:
> and behold the banker instantly concealed in the bank parlour!"[7]

There has been a critical tendency to group "The Piper at the Gates of Dawn" with "Wayfarers All," and, as we have seen, there is some structural and symbolic sense in doing so. But the very different styles of the two chapters demonstrate clearly that one is inward-looking, the other outward-looking; the first is self-consciously "fey," the second much closer to Richard Jefferies's tough observation of the natural world. Both chapters may conjure a dream of another world, but the world of "Wayfarers All" is very solid and specific.

"Wayfarers All" is perhaps the chapter that best fits Peter Green's claims for "good prose." In this virtuoso performance Grahame conjures up the air of an idyllically warm late summer and Mediterranean ports, and of the Sea Rat's mesmeric call. He relies on sensual but concrete details, and on rhythm and pace rather than on personification or highly coloured words: "the salmon leap on the flood tide, schools of mackerel flash and play past quay-sides and foreshores, and by the windows the great vessels glide, night and day, up to their moorings or forth to the open sea" (172).

Also interesting about "Wayfarers All" is the way in which the conversation between the two Rats is balanced between direct and indirect speech—and what direct speech there is, is curiously formal. Here Grahame uses language with great skill to avoid troublesome interactions of several kinds; it is a language of evasion, but, paradoxically, it holds the book together by reflecting its many moods and levels.

THE LANGUAGE OF EVASION

"Yes, it's *the* life, the only life, to live," responded the Water Rat dreamily, and without his usual wholehearted conviction.

"I did not say exactly that," replied the stranger cautiously. . . . (162–63)

The fact that *The Wind in the Willows* coheres at all depends upon the way the language operates at certain crucial points. One of the most spectacular examples is Toad's first solo adventure, in which he steals a car and is caught, tried, and sent to the gaol. W. W. Robson has observed that "the authorial or editorial voice seems to have gone slightly crazy" in this sequence, and Carpenter comments that it "suggests uneasiness of authorial control."[8] I would argue the exact opposite: had Grahame not manipulated various styles, the book would not work.

The problem is to take Toad from the animal world to the human world, from the animal arcadia where he is child/animal/squire to the situation where Toad the "human" is confronting the law of the "real," human world. Rather than moving from "play" to "reality" directly, Grahame shifts from relatively naturalistic writing to parody and farce, via Toad's egocentric, childish, perhaps sexual escape. . . . "Fulfilling his instincts, living his hour, reckless of what might come to him" (113). This collision of child and adult frenzy is, in true Jerome K. Jerome style, abruptly halted, and we are thrown into a different world, a comic opera, Gilbert and Sullivan police court:

> "To my mind," observed the Chairman of the Bench of Magistrates cheerfully, "the *only* difficulty that presents itself in this otherwise very clear case is, how we can possibly make it sufficiently hot for the incorrigible rogue and hardened ruffian whom we see cowering in the dock before us." (113)

Grahame cannot afford to see (as Jan Needle did) Toad as anything but a figure of farce: had he done so, the sociological implications would be overwhelming. Grahame slips a little toward the end of the book, by drifting a little too close to realism, when Rat observes to Toad that "no criminal laws had ever been known to prevail against cheek and plausibility such as yours, combined with the power of a long purse" (204), but his description of the court is much more surefooted. Toad, it should be observed, does not speak.

The magistrate's court, illustrated with masterstrokes by Shepard (114–15), demonstrates by its vastly disproportionate sentence ("It's going to be twenty years for you this time" [114]) that the human world is as eccentric as the animals' is sane—or that the adult world is madder than the children's is. From that premise, there is nowhere to go except into farce, and Grahame produces probably the best parody of the gothic style ever written. The great gothic novels, such as Horace Walpole's *The Castle of Otranto* (1764) and Ann Radcliffe's *The Mysteries of Udolpho* (1794) set a fashion that survived through writers like Harrison Ainsworth (who flourished in the 1840s with novels such as *Old St. Paul's*) and had become part of the popular culture of the "penny dreadful" by the end of the century. One characteristic example might be the anonymous "The String of Pearls," a version of the story of Sweeny Todd, the demon barber, which appeared in the *People's Periodical and Family Library* in 1846:

> Whatever unhappy wretch reads these lines may bid adieu to the world and all hope, for he is a doomed man! He will never emerge from these vaults with life, for there is a secret so hideous that to write it makes one's blood curdle and the flesh to creep upon your bones.[9]

The trappings of dungeons and horrid mysteries were, of course, exploited by Poe, and they are still alive in film and popular literature. Grahame's version is a tour de force, as Toad moves rapidly backward both through time and through literary convention to the sergeant of police: "'Oddsbodikins! . . . Rouse thee, old loon . . . '" (116).

If this shift of style is necessary at a major crux in the book, so it is also important in small encounters. At one extreme, there is the narrative paraphrase of speech, as in Otter's first meeting with Mole, where Grahame simply evades the difficult problems of interclass communication. At the other there is Toad's encounter with the engine-driver, in a scene that echoes another in *Three Men in a Boat*. Here Grahame is dealing not only with the animal-human divide but also with the class divide.

When Toad first encounters the engine-driver, who thinks him to be a washerwoman, the engine-driver (perhaps a little patronizingly called the "good" engine-driver) speaks naturally enough at first: "You're a washerwoman to your trade, says you. Very well, that's that. And I'm an engine-driver, as you may well see, and there's no denying it's terribly dirty work. Uses up a power of shirts, it does" (148). It should be noted, though, that this is a response to Toad's having spoken "in character." Just as when the barge-woman throws Toad off the barge, they have spoken—but not conversed—in their natural dialect, so with the engine-driver. However, as the driver looks over the back of the engine and sees the motley crew in the pursuing engine, Grahame shifts the language back to that of comic opera, simultaneously solving his problem of interclass communication. Toad is revealed as from a different world (in various ways):

> The engine-driver looked very grave and said, "I fear that you have been indeed a wicked toad, and by rights I ought to give you up to offended justice. But you are evidently in sore trouble and distress, so I will not desert you." (151)

Two comparisons of technique are instructive. The first might be with one of Grahame's contemporaries, Edith Nesbit. Nesbit was one of the first members of the Fabian Society; although this social conscience does not often show directly in her books, it does show indirectly in her approach to the contact between the middle classes and the working classes, for she is able to confront these class distinctions directly. In *The Railway Children*, she presents several interactions between middle-class children and working-class characters, and she is meticulous that the working-classes should use dialect—and the children very often innocently echo them. Bobbie, for example, having attempted to get the engine-driver to mend her brother's toy train, finds herself on an engine:

> "I thought," she said wistfully, "that perhaps you'd mend this for me—because you're an engineer, you know."
> The engine-driver said he was blowed if he wasn't blest.
> "I'm blessed if I ain't blowed," remarked the fireman. . . . "It's like your precious cheek," said the engine driver "whatever made you think we'd be bothered tinkering penny toys?"
> "I didn't mean it for precious cheek," said Bobbie; "only everybody that has anything to do with railways is so kind and good, I didn't think you'd mind. You don't really—do you?"[10]

Class interactions occur throughout *The Wind in the Willows*, but, as might be expected, we rarely hear the working classes speak for themselves (hedgehogs and field mice are the most eloquent). One of the finer features of Jan Needle's *Wild Wood* is the fact that we rarely hear the riverbankers—and the narrator, Baxter ferret, uses exactly Grahame's distancing technique. One notable exception is when Baxter confronts Toad after a car crash:

> "We've come for the waggon. 'Tis the gaffer's," . . .
>
> "Good men, good men [said Toad]. Tow the old warhorse back to rest, eh? Just the fellows I wanted to meet. Give me the . . . er . . . gaffer's name if you'd be so kind so that I can get in touch and settle the account with him."
>
> I saw a glimmer of hope through my misery. Took my courage in both hands. Spoke to the gentleman.
>
> "Would you be saying. . . ? I mean, does that allow you . . . ?"
>
> . . . It was no use. I was in a new world, a different world. *I didn't even know how to speak the same language.*[11]

Generally, a style that "tells" rather than "shows," that uses indirect, reported speech rather than direct, quoted speech, implies more control (or attempted control) on the part of the author-narrator. Grahame, in negotiating the difficulties of class and and interpersonal relationships evades the difficulties that would ensue from direct interaction. A. A. Milne, when he came to adapt *The Wind in the Willows* as *Toad of Toad Hall*, could not afford such obliqueness; he was forced, through obvious dramatic necessity, to transfer this indirect speech to direct speech. Fortunately for him, he was generally—by conscious choice—operating with only the farcical elements. But the comparison of Milne's treatment of the scene involving Toad, the gaoler's daughter, and her aunt demonstrates just how sophisticated is the style of *The Wind in the Willows*, in the sense of acting at one remove from a child audience; it also neatly illustrates Milne's method.

> . . . the only stipulation the old lady made being that she should be gagged and bound and dumped down in a corner. By this not very convincing artifice, she explained, aided by picturesque fic-

tion which she could supply herself, she hoped to retain her situation, in spite of the suspicious appearance of things.

Toad was delighted with the suggestion. It would enable him to leave the prison in some style, and with his reputation for being a desperate and dangerous fellow untarnished; and he readily helped the gaoler's daughter to make her aunt appear as much as possible the victim of circumstances over which she had no control (140–41).

In *Toad of Toad Hall*, on the other hand, the Aunt is a solid comic character, and the gaoler's daughter has acquired a name, Phoebe. Both of these changes can be seen as comments on Grahame's attitudes toward women, as well as to his audience.

AUNT. You told him the condition?

TOAD. Condition?

PHOEBE. My aunt thinks she ought to be gagged and bound, so as to look as if she had been overcome. You'd like it, too. You wanted to leave the prison in style.

TOAD. (*beamingly*). An excellent idea! So such more in keeping with my character.

AUNT. I brought a bit of rope along, in case like.

TOAD. Splendid!

AUNT. (*enjoying it*). Got a nankerchief?

TOAD. (*producing one*). Yes.

AUNT. Then you gags me first. (*In a hoarse whisper*) Help! Help! Help! Help!

TOAD. (*carried away by the realism of this*). Silence, woman, else I gag thee!

AUNT. (*undeterred*). Help! Help! Help!

TOAD. (*advancing with gag*). Thou hast brought it on thyself . . . A murrain on thy cackling tongue![12]

There is one other stylistic feature of the dialogue in *The Wind in the Willows* that brings us back to both characters and class. Our four heroes generally speak a standard middle-class English with characteristic idioms of the period. In the first two chapters Rat uses the expressions "my young friend," "Look here," "Hold hard a minute," "you silly ass," and "Thanks awfully"; Toad says, "Now what will you take?" and Otter calls his friends "Greedy beggars." It is Badger who presents problems, linguistically speaking, for his "common" way of speaking seems slightly out of place with his obvious commanding position of class. Is he a squire? An old eccentric lord? Or a portrait of Furnivall, "a wild man of letters . . . a natural odd man out"?[13] Once again, the language, as it were, twists and turns, unsettling our images of the characters.

> The Toad, having finished his breakfast, picked up a stout stick and swung it vigorously, belabouring imaginary animals. "I'll learn 'em to steal my house!" he cried. "I'll learn 'em, I'll learn 'em!"
>
> "Don't say 'learn 'em,' Toad," said the Rat, greatly shocked. "It's not good English."
>
> "What are you always nagging at Toad for?" inquired the Badger rather peevishly. "What's the matter with his English? It's the same as what I use myself, and if it's good enough for me, it ought to be good enough for you!"
>
> "I'm very sorry," said the Rat humbly. "Only I *think* it ought to be 'teach 'em', not 'learn 'em'."
>
> "But we don't *want* to teach 'em," replied the Badger. "We want to *learn 'em*—learn 'em, learn 'em! And what's more, we're going to *do* it, too!"
>
> "O, very well, have it your own way," said the Rat. He was getting rather muddled about it himself, and presently retired into a corner where he could be heard muttering, "Learn 'em, teach 'em, learn 'em, teach 'em!" till the Badger told him rather sharply to leave off. (218)

Badger, as identified by his language use, represents many facets of a cultural center point: he is above (or rather beneath) society; he is the father figure that Grahame was looking for, the earthy stability that could empathize with the child in freedom of speech—who was common in a way that made him one with the Moles and the Hedgehogs, yet unchallengeable in a way that made him one with the middle-classes.

Even more than in the case of the river, or the god Pan, or the Sea Rat, there is a linguistic riddle surrounding Badger, which, as with so much of the style of *The Wind in the Willows*, seems calculated to unsettle the reader.

THE LANGUAGE OF LITERATURE

[A]nd with his ear to the reed-stems he caught, at intervals, something of what the wind went whispering so constantly among them. (21)

Kenneth Grahame was a man of considerable literary sophistication, and it is not surprising that many commentators have noticed the density of allusion in *The Wind in the Willows*. Of course, only a few will recognize the wealth of literary reference that Peter Green, for example, identifies:

> Kenneth Grahame was a well-read and essentially bookish man, with a taste for quotation . . . and overt or covert parody. Some of the jokes, like borrowing a line from Tennyson's "Home they brought her warrior dead" to provide the lachrymose Toad with a chapter-title, delight by their sheer incongruity.[14]

Yet there remains a coherence about the materials from which, in a sense, *The Wind in the Willows* is composed.

It is not surprising that Grahame's affinity with the Romantic poets has recently been noted.[15] Grahame, in general terms, combines the freshness of Keatsean romantic imagery with the rather overblown *fin-de-siècle* atmospherics of his contemporaries; he is in the political tradition of the later Wordsworth, rather than of the revolutionary Shelley. Perhaps most striking is "Wayfarers All," where the description of the Sea Rat has several verbal echoes of Coleridge's Ancient Mariner, and the Water Rat becomes as mesmerized as was the wedding guest. Similarly, the atmosphere that Grahame builds up is in much the same tone as the lush language of Keats's odes.

Mole's emergence into the sunlight in chapter 1 is at least reminiscent of Wordsworth's "The Prelude." Where for Mole "The sunshine struck hot on his fur, soft breezes caressed his heated brow" (1–2), Wordsworth's great poem begins, "O there is blessing in this gentle breeze / A visitant that while he fans my cheek / Doth seem half-conscious of the joy he brings / From the green fields, and from yon azure sky." (I.1.4) It echoes as well the greatest moment of revelation in the poem, when in book 14 he writes, ". . . instantly a light upon the turf / Fell like a flash." (xiv. 38–9)

Similarly, Lesley Willis detects echoes of Blake, and Richard Gillin finds echoes of Wordsworth in "The Piper at the Gates of Dawn." However, rather than identifying specific echoes or borrowings, it might be better to note simply that Grahame was working at the end of a tradition that, via Tennyson and the later Victorian poets, had arrived at a rather insubstantial, artificial romantic style. Thus, a text of such density and conscious craftsmanship, with multiple literary echoes if not precise references, is only to be expected.

If there are echoes of Homer in the tale of Toad, with his self-praise, the arming ceremony, and the triumphant return, there are also classical echoes in Grahame's attempt to resolve the sexual ambiguities of the child-in-the-adult. "The most natural path to a happy, asexual world," notes Geraldine Poss, "is the path back to childhood." Consequently, in a classical arcadian tradition, Grahame's animals "eliminate desire altogether."[16] And if there are traces of the "Uncle Remus" stories, or of Beatrix Potter's heroes, there are even stronger traces of the sophisticated humor of the Grossmiths and Jerome K. Jerome.

But among the parodies and allusions, and within this dense texture, there contrives to be a text of great originality. The question remains, who is it *for?*

8

"A Book for Youth"

"Here, you two youngsters be off home to your mother," said the Badger kindly. "I'll send someone with you to show you the way." (70)

On the cover of one American edition of *The Wind in the Willows* (Aladdin Books), published eighty-one years after its first appearance, are the words, in very small print: ALL AGES. The book has been known, and presumably loved, as a children's book for most of those years—surely, then, it would be merely an academic affectation to question whether it is really a children's book at all? And yet, looking past the superficial trappings of an animal story to the narrative structure, the symbolism, and the language, there seems to be little that is *intended* for a child readership.

The book's opening lines—"The Mole had been working very hard all the morning, spring cleaning his little home"—seem to be directed at children. There is one incident when the narrator seems to be addressing children more or less directly, over the question of manners:

> The Badger did not mind that sort of thing at all, nor did he take any notice of elbows on the table, or everyone speaking at once. As he did not go into Society himself, he had got an idea that these things belonged to the things that didn't really matter. (We know of course that he was wrong, and took too narrow a view; because they do matter very much, though it would take too long to explain why.) (62)

But beyond that . . . ?

In this discussion of *The Wind in the Willows*, we have seen three general ways of approaching the book. The first involves the idea that it is two very different books, one for children and one for adults, spliced together; the second, that the book's density makes it inescapably an adult's book, while the anthropomorphism makes it seem like a child's book; the third, that it is clearly a children's book, and that any other status has been forced upon it by the colonizing impulses of symbol-hunting adults. For a fourth, Barbara Wall has suggested that the whole book is a smokescreen: "It was because Rat and Mole were firmly fixed as characters in a children's story, and therefore in a sense not to be taken too seriously, that they could safely be used in episodes dealing with the author's own imperfectly understood longings."[1]

For purposes of clarity, it would be useful at this stage to consider just how a children's book might be defined, and how far *The Wind in the Willows* conforms to the definition. As W. W. Robson has observed, one reason why the book is on the edge of the established canon of literature is "partly due to the uncertainty about whether or not the book is children's literature." He goes on, "My answer is no—unless you mean by children's literature one of those books which are ineffective unless the child in the reader responds to the child in the author."[2]

Of course, there is no simple answer to what children's literature is; perhaps ideally it is a literature *of* childhood and *for* childhood in the sense that there is no intrusive adult control or mediation of the story and its telling. That, of course, is an impossibility, but there are obviously degrees of control; we might deduce how "childist" or "adultist" a writer is from his or her narrative stance. C. S. Lewis, for example, betrays by his controlling and paternalistic tones a certain disrespect for his audience in his "Narnia" series; Enid Blyton, probably the world's biggest-selling children's author, tends to merge the narrative voice with the characters' viewpoints. As might be expected, the narrative stance of *The Wind in the Willows* presents certain problems in this respect.

In Barbara Wall's extremely useful taxonomy, children's books can be characterized by "single," "dual," or "double" address. Her explanation is worth examining at some length, as it could be brought to bear, to good effect, on much work that might be done with children's literature. The single address, as used by Arthur Ransome, speaks directly to children; the double address talks to them, but also looks over their heads, very often winking at the adults (as in Barrie or Milne), and, by implication, downgrading the contract between author and child reader. The most common, most well-accepted type of writing, uses a dual address "in a way that allows adult narrator and child narratee a conjunction of interests."[3] In this light, Wall's comments on *The Wind in the Willows* are very interesting. Her general view is that, unlike the skillful craftsmanship of Kipling,

> Grahame . . . seems to be unaware of his uncertain stance. He does not oscillate between stances for artistic reasons, but because he has never seen the book as a whole. . . . Grahame's particular variety of double address, in which the narrator shows no consciousness at all of an implied child reader for chapters at a time, surprisingly, is seldom criticised.[4]

Unfortunately, this is a kind of sophistication is not often to be found in criticism of the book or of children's literature generally. Instead, there has been a much more simplistic tendency to gauge children's literature by a limited number of more superficial features. Myles Macdowell's effort to define children's literature is a good example:

[C]hildren's books are generally shorter; they tend to favour an active rather than passive treatment, with dialogue and incident rather than description and introspection; child protagonists are the rule; conventions are much used; the story develops within a clear-cut moral schematism which much adult fiction ignores; children's books tend to be optimistic rather than depressive; language is child-oriented; plots are of a distinctive order. . . .[5]

Clearly, *The Wind in the Willows* does not fit very comfortably into Macdowell's thinking—though, as we have seen, it has given many critics analogous problems. Some of his categories can describe Toad's adventures (they are active and full of incidents), but the converse is also true. The book's overall moral scheme is ambiguous, and ultimately it is difficult to say whether the book is optimistic or depressive. The language, as we have seen, is not generally oriented toward childhood at all (which, however, is not to deny that the language forms part of the book's appeal). And while the book's plots may fit neatly into a distinctive order, or orders, they nevertheless clash with each other.

Conventionally speaking, the animal characters mark *The Wind in the Willows* as a children's book, as do the prominent themes and symbols of comfort, security, the search for a father, rebellion, and egocentrism. The book's *Bildungsroman* elements, however, shift it into a different category—that of the adolescent novel. Equally, of course, these elements can all be seen as representing a regressive side of adulthood; so they are two sides of the same coin. Specific elements may also be approached from, as it were, two sides, such as the preoccupation with food. The wonderful food orgy of Rat's wicker basket is not soon forgotten by any reader:

coldtonguecoldhamcoldbeefpickledgherkinssalad-
frenchrollscresssandwidgespottedmeatgingerbeerlemonadeso-
dawater— (7)

There are many things that will please, and obviously have pleased, the child, but as we have seen, this kind of material may "stand in" for less innocent concerns: food, notably, might be related to sexuality, which still lurks in the background.

But are these two ways of approaching the book incompatible? Can a book, in other words, be *simultaneously* a children's book and an adult's book? In part, the confusion over the book arises because so many of the features that appear to make *The Wind in the Willows* a children's book are coterminous with the pleasures of childhood. If *The Wind in the Willows* is in one sense the world of the adult in retreat, we should not assume that the return to childhood is a return to simplemindedness. In the matter of food, for example, Grahame is, as it were, having his cake and eating it too: not only is there a metaphoric-symbolic aspect to food, but there is a literal delight—which, as C. S. Lewis, a writer sometimes said to be influenced by Grahame, has observed, is *not* a sign of arrested development:

> But surely arrested development consists not in refusing to lose old things but in failing to add new things? I now like hock, which I am sure I should not have liked as a child. But I still like lemon squash.[6]

This is the positive side of the book's ambiguous position. Its negative side leads to dangerous confusions. The most notable of these center around its nostalgic-arcadian element. What Grahame is creating is, on the one hand, a playground without responsibility, and we might well assume that generations of children have been led into it. He is, of course, also creating a regressive idyll: this is the "secret garden" of adult consciousness, the arcadia that never was, where adults can escape to food and games, a place "clean of the clash of sex." As Margaret Meek pithily puts it:

> Young readers meet a storyteller of distinct verbal felicity, in parts, but of clearly limited range for modern children. The excitement of reading is a dialogue with their future. Here they encounter the author's imagined past. For a time it may prove delightful, even re-creative. But this arcadian world is neither brave nor new.[7]

The playgrounds are therefore the same area but approached from different ways; but the worm in the bud, as far as children are concerned, is that *The Wind in the Willows* offers not growth or escape but only *return* and repression. The Rat, most notably, has lived only in one place, knows nothing else, and (except for a moment of madness) wants nothing else. The Mole, having moved so far, wistfully would like to go on, but is held back. The wide world is forbidden—except to dangerous eccentrics such as the Sea Rat, ethereal beings such as the swallows, and social deviants such as Toad. And, in the case of Toad, all the weight of adult repression is soon marshaled—so that, in a remarkable passage of sublimated sexuality, we have the uncomfortable spectacle of the adult playing as a frustrated child—and, simultaneously, of the child being frustrated:

> When his violent paroxysms possessed him he would arrange bedroom chairs in rude resemblance of a motor-car and would crouch on the foremost of them, bent forward and staring fixedly ahead, making uncouth and ghastly noises, till the climax was reached, when, turning a complete somersault, he would lie prostrate amidst the ruins of the chairs, apparently completely satisfied for the moment. (105)

Thus, for all its apparent appeal, it could be said that *The Wind in the Willows* represents an unfashionable, perhaps unedifying, aspect of adulthood. To the child it offers only limitations: it does not confront, rather, it continually confirms—it is inward-looking rather than outgoing.

Of course, it could be argued that this is precisely what children *want* at some stages of their development, and that they are as likely to read the book for comfort as is an adult. This may well be true; but if it is, there seems to be something of a mismatch between the implied structures and "shape" of the story and the implied audience.

If, on the other hand, one argues that a book so obviously written for adults could not possibly have been so misinterpreted for so long, one could—apart from citing other oddities such as William Golding's *Lord of the Flies* being prescribed for generations of children, or *Jane Eyre* being regarded as an adult, rather than an adolescent classic—note the importance of adult prescription, marketing, and intention upon the child audience. What happens in reality, is that the book has been and is read only *partially* (A. A. Milne's *Winnie-the-Pooh* is another example). A contemporary (Canadian) critic, Michele Landsberg, has commented, "An adult reading aloud might judiciously choose to omit the central chapter with its vision of Pan, a passage whose religious effulgence tips the book's delicate balance of ironic humour and calm affections. I remember skipping past those intensely embarrassing pages when I was a child."[8] But who is embarrassed—the child that was, the adult that is, the child who is remembered, the child-in-the adult?—and what is she or he embarrassed about? To say that *parts* of a book appeal to a child brings almost all books into the category of children's literature.

This examination of *The Wind in the Willows* may, in fact, bring us up against an unpalatable truth: that the "great children's books" are those most like adult books—adults choose the canon by adult criteria, and children follow. It is obvious that children must be educated into "good taste," and that the "good" book, as recognized by childhood may well be unrecognizable by the adult world. And where it does exist, it is disapproved of. In assessing *The Wind in the Willows* and its place in our culture, then, we have to see past what might be generations of misunderstanding. Just as the fairy tale sits very uncomfortably in the nursery, so the appropriate shelf for *The Wind in the Willows* is not obvious. Indeed, the kind of cozy, reminiscing, protective tone that many contemporary (and casual) critics use when talking about the book might well arouse suspicion.

And there, perhaps, lies the secret, and the identity of *The Wind in the Willows*: it is a manipulative book, providing not only social harmony for adults but social conditioning for children. Those elements that, in *Alice's Adventures in Wonderland*, suggest that the child can be a free spirit and judge the adult world, and be untouched, unviolated by it, are here inverted. The assumption that the life of the riverbankers is a good one is in fact highly political: conservatism is not neutral.

But, equally, it might be argued that *The Wind in the Willows* actually contains tensions between rebellion and conservatism. The

Mole may go no further than the riverbank, the Rat may give up his dreams of the sun, the Toad may sing his songs in private—but they *do* yearn, and they *do* dream, and they *do* sing. Is not this a form of reality—telling children the truth, that life is limited?

The Wind in the Willows, then, is one of the splendid paradoxes of English literature. In theory, it is difficult to see many ways in which it can be described as a children's book; in practice, though, it works very well as one. If anything, we might be concerned not so much with the effect of the book upon children as with the fact that it has not been sufficiently appreciated by adults. The "children's book" label has led to adults reading *The Wind in the Willows* in a certain way; the way in which I have approached it has perhaps required a shift of attitude.

My own feeling is that, as an adult, I can read *The Wind in the Willows* both as the remembered child and as the suppressed child; my reading now blurs with my reading then. My nostalgia for a less-crowded riverbank tends to collide with my ideal of what a riverbank should be, an ideal generated by reading *The Wind in the Willows* forty years ago. This is not an uncommon feature of rereading—but with *The Wind in the Willows* the ideal of the future blends with the ideal of the golden past. There is a tension in this, but it is a creative tension. Grahame's comment that it is "a book for youth" was as perceptive as—or perhaps perceptive because—it was ambiguous.

A. A. Milne, recommending *The Wind in the Willows* as "a household book," took a reverential and sentimental stance, but for all that, his final words are worth serious consideration:

> But I must give you one word of warning. When you sit down to [*The Wind in the Willows*], don't be so ridiculous as to suppose that you are sitting in judgement on my taste, still less on the genius of Kenneth Grahame. You are merely sitting in judgement on yourself. . . . You may be worthy; I do not know. But it is you who are on trial.[9]

9

Approaches to Teaching

"I can make you comfortable. And I'll teach you to row, and to swim, and you'll soon be as handy on the water as any of us." (21)

The Wind in the Willows, because of its ambiguous status between adults' and children's books, its many styles and symbols, and its precise historical location, is an excellent book from which to explore many aspects of literature and society, politics, symbolism, and history. This exploration can be made at virtually any level, from high school to graduate school. Such is the versatility of the text: the only differentiating factor is the depth of study.

There is no shortage of books that present classroom strategies for teaching literature,[1] so this chapter will suggest paths that can be followed rather than techniques to employ. All the ensuing suggestions can be pursued individually or in groups, in classroom situations or in private study, as short sessions or longer-term projects, as oral discussion or written report.

In all cases *The Wind in the Willows* provides either a starting point, a reference point, or a central source.

Children's Literature in General

One of the key themes of this present work has been whether *The Wind in the Willows* can be considered to be children's book. This raises wider issues, most of which can be explored from local experience.

1. The first question, which may seem to be easy at first is, what is a children's book?[2]

2. This leads rapidly to the question: What is a child? The way in which concepts of childhood have changed—from one period to another, from place to place, among different races and social classes—can be explored. How childhood is conceptualized makes a good deal of difference to what kinds of books are written for children.

3. What are the characteristics of style that you would expect to find, or that you actually do find, in books sold or classified as children's books? If style is supposed to be "simple," just what does "simple" actually mean?

4. What are the characteristics of content? This opens up a wide area: What do we find in children's books, what do we *not* find, and what *should* we find? *The Wind in the Willows*, for example, does not deal with sexuality, but it does deal with an all-male society. In the 1990s the emphasis on food and drink (and tobacco smoking) is no longer the happy and innocent thing it once was. The exploration of this topic can (and perhaps should) lead to a discussion of censorship.

5. Are there topics that should be left out of, or censored or suppressed in, children's books? Who decides—who should decide? What do you approve of, and how does a personal opinion relate to society?[3]

The status of *The Wind in the Willows*, whether it is a children's book or not, is very ambiguous. However, this status is far from unique: a good many books have found themselves in this no-person's-land, and it is interesting to compile a list. Central to the discussion might be Mark Twain's *Huckleberry Finn*, Alan Garner's *Red Shift* and *The Stone Book Quartet*, Cynthia Voight's "Tillerman" books (such as *Homecoming* [1981] and *Dicey's Song* [1982]), Judy Blume's *Forever*,

Russell Hoban's *The Mouse and His Child*, and J. R. R. Tolkien's *The Lord of the Rings*. In recent years in Britain, two children's books, K. M. Peyton's *Flambards* and Anne Fine's *My War with Goggle-Eyes*, have been made into prime-time adult TV mini-series. Are there any other examples, and what does this ambivalence imply?

Two ways of distinguishing between books for children and books for adults have been suggested in earlier chapters: the shape of the narrative, and the narrative stance of the author/narrator. It is good literary practice to chart the plot shapes and the tones of voice that various narrators adopt in a very wide range of books—from picture books to adult novels, and from popular fiction to "classics." The results are often quite surprising, particularly with picture books and "teenage" fiction. Consider, for example, the clash in many "young adult" books between the "adult" themes and the very comforting, "resolved" plot shapes.

Another, related confusion, results from the use of fantasy. Is this for adults or children? In the modern world, is it irresponsible to "retreat" into fantasy, or is it necessary to maintain a healthy imagination? (Also, to what extent are the answers to these questions ideologically rooted?) Or, as in *The Wind in the Willows*, does the use of talking animals and other fantasy features give authors the chance to say something more profound than appears on the surface?

It is fruitful to explore the ways in which talking animals are used in *The Wind in the Willows* as well as in many other children's books and in adult satires. One step onward from this is to consider whether the fairy tale should be read by children—and, if it should not, by whom shuld it be read? Ursula K. le Guin has asked: "Why are Americans afraid of dragons?" on the principle that "something that goes very deep in the American character [is] a moral disapproval of fantasy, a disapproval so intense, and often so aggressive, that I cannot help but see it as arising, fundamentally, from fear."[4] Where does this attitude stem from?

THE WIND IN THE WILLOWS AND LITERARY EXPLORATIONS

The Wind in the Willows is set very firmly in a particular country and time, and, within that, in a particular social structure. What difference does this make to the way readers respond to it?

1. Are there any elements of *The Wind in the Willows* that are difficult to understand?

2. The animals speak a very distinctive dialect. Can it be identified, and can a vocabulary/glossary be developed?

3. Historically, *The Wind in the Willows* is concerned with very specific problems of social change and unrest—but to what extent are they universal? It is interesting to take Grahame's fears and relate them to today—are there parallels? Are the same problems still around? Aidan Chambers, writing about Richard Adams's animal fantasy, *Watership Down*, said that it was "what one might expect had *The Wind in the Willows* been written after two world wars . . . [the] nuclear bomb, the Korean and Vietnam obscenities and half a dozen other hells created by the inexhaustibly evil powers of man."[5] Is it true that *The Wind in the Willows* is far too gentle, far too restrained, to be relevant to today?

Another important aspect of *The Wind in the Willows*, and, indeed, of much literature, is its symbolism. Grahame's book is an excellent starting point for an exploration of how symbolism works, both in literature and in general.

A good place to start is the river. What has it meant in practical terms, and what has it meant more deeply to people in different places and different times? To the British, it tends to mean security; the Nile in Egypt, which alone made arable the valley through which it runs, was considered to be a god; the Mississippi, in a book like *Huckleberry Finn* might mean the frontier, or escape, or cleansing. A similar assembling of symbolic meanings is illuminating, perhaps especially when they clash with each other and with personal interpretations.

This leads us to consider what (other) critical approaches are appropriate to *The Wind in the Willows*. One line of investigation might be a "feminist" one. What attitudes toward women does the book present, and if it they are essentially negative, what does this mean for the ways teaching of the book in schools—indeed for the distribution of the book generally?

The position of women in society was under discussion in Grahame's time as much as it is now, and so *The Wind in the Willows* might also be examined in its literary and historical contexts. Is it typical of its time? What was going on in adult literature and children's literature? Was Grahame right to be worried?

And finally, as with all literature, it is very important not to overlook or dismiss personal responses; *The Wind in the Willows* is a particularly rich text in the sense that it relates to many parts of childhood, adolescence, and adulthood in very emotive ways. To consider which parts of the book made the greatest impression on readers, and how those reactions relate to the readers' personal histories can deepen understanding of how literature works.

THE WIND IN THE WILLOWS AND CREATIVE WRITING

One increasingly popular way of teaching literature is to use the central text as a basis for new writing. We have seen the way in which *The Wind in the Willows* led to Milne's play, *Toad of Toad Hall*, and Jan Needle's *Wild Wood*, and these ideas can be extended.

1. *The Wind in the Willows* has a specific English background. Could it be transplanted to, say, a North American river? What differences would this make to the plot, especially if new animal personae were chosen?

2. Could the plot be transplanted to the 1990s? What would be the situation of Mole, Rat, Badger, and Toad in a society that has changed so radically—especially as regards things like automobile and the social status of women?

3. Could the story be continued, either in the context of 1908 or 1998? Would Mole move on? Would the Chief Weasel take revenge? Would Toad relapse?

4. Could the story be retold from yet another angle? For example, would Rat's housekeeper or Mole's char-mouse have stories to tell? What

about the shopkeepers who stay open in the festive season, or the schoolmaster in the Wild Wood? Grahame's "character economy" leaves a good many gaps to be filled.

All these "creative" devices bring students into close contact not only with the texture of the novel but also with the technical problems of writing.

THE WIND IN THE WILLOWS AND OTHER MEDIA

Another popular teaching device is the comparison of a text with its other versions. This can involve the study of illustration, as well as various adaptations—film and video, for example. It also focuses on how individual one's interpretation of a text is, and how far the book "itself" can survive in other media.

The Wind in the Willows, as a book to stimulate literary investigation, suffers from an embarrassment of riches; it has a lot to offer, and teachers could do worse than consider the sage, if ungrammatical, words of the Badger:

> "But we don't *want* to teach 'em. . . . We want to *learn 'em*, learn 'em, learn 'em! And what's more, we're going to *do* it, too!" (218)

Notes and References

2. The Importance of the Work

1. Neil Philip, "Kenneth Grahame's *The Wind in the Willows*: A Companionable Vitality," in *Touchstones: Reflections on the Best in Children's Literature*, edited by Perry Nodelman (West Lafayette, Ind.: Children's Literature Association, 1985), 104.

2. A. A. Milne, "A Household Book," in *Not That It Matters* (London: Methuen, 1920), 88–89.

3. Patrick R. Chalmers, *Kenneth Grahame: Life, Letters and Unpublished Work* (London: Methuen, 1933), 139–41.

4. Lois Kuznets, *Kenneth Grahame* (Boston: Twayne, 1987), 122.

5. *The Wind in the Willows*, retold for easy reading by Joan Collins (Loughborough, Eng.: Ladybird Books, 1983), 2.

6. Tony Watkins, "'Making a Break for the Real England': The River-Bankers Revisited," *Children's Literature Association Quarterly*, 9, no. 1 (Spring 1984): 34–35.)

7. Margery Fisher, *Classics for Children and Young People* (South Woodchester, Eng.: The Thimble Press, 1986), 37.

8. Lois Kuznets, *Kenneth Grahame*, 121.

3. The Critical Reception

1. Sir Paul Harvey, *The Oxford Companion to English Literature* 4th ed. (Oxford: Oxford University Press, 1969), 346.

2. Quoted in Chalmers, *Kenneth Grahame*, 90.

3. Chalmers, *Kenneth Grahame*, 91–92.

4. Ibid., 139–40.

5. Quoted in ibid., 127.

6. *Punch*, 135 (11 Nov. 1908), 360, quoted in Peter Green, *Kenneth Grahame: A Biography* (London: John Murray, 1959), 256, 258.

7. *Saturday Review of Literature*, 106 (12 December 1908), quoted in Peter Green, *Kenneth Grahame*, 256.

8. *Nation*, 4, 10 (5 Dec. 1908), 404, quoted in Peter Green, *Kenneth Grahame*, 256.

9. *The New Age* (24 Oct. 1908), reprinted in *Books and Persons* (1917), 57–59, quoted in Peter Green, *Kenneth Grahame*, 258.

10. Quoted in Chalmers, *Kenneth Grahame*, 127–28.

11. *The Bookman* (January 1909), 190–91, quoted in Peter Green, *Kenneth Grahame*, 257.

12. Cited by Juliet Dusinberre, *Alice to the Lighthouse* (London: Macmillan, 1987), 279n2.

13. Chalmers, *Kenneth Grahame*, 127.

14. A. A. Milne, *Toad of Toad Hall* (London: Methuen, 1931), v–vi.

15. Quoted by Roger Lancelyn Green, *Tellers of Tales*, 2nd ed. (London: Edmund Ward, 1953), 234.

16. Elizabeth Cripps, "Kenneth Grahame: Children's Author?" *Children's Literature in Education* 12 (1981): 15–23; Mary Haynes, "*The Wind in the Willows*—A Classic for Children?" *International Review of Children's Literature and Librarianship*, 4, no. 2 (1989), 115–29.

17. W. W. Robson, "On *The Wind in the Willows*," in *The Definition of Literature and Other Essays* (Cambridge: Cambridge University Press, 1982), 143.

18. Humphrey Carpenter, *Secret Gardens* (London: Unwin Hyman, 1987), 168.

19. Roger Lancelyn Green, *Tellers of Tales*, 232.

20. Chalmers, *Kenneth Grahame*, 138.

21. Peter Green, *Kenneth Grahame*, 244–45.

22. Peter Green, *Kenneth Grahame*, 251.

23. Clifton Fadiman, "Professionals and Confessionals: Dr Seuss and Kenneth Grahame," in *Only Connect: Readings on Children's Literature*, edited by Sheila Egoff, G. T. Stubbs, and L. F. Ashley, 2nd ed. (Toronto: Oxford University Press, 1980), 280.

24. Geraldine D. Poss, "An Epic in Arcadia: The Pastoral World of *The Wind in the Willows*," *Children's Literature 4* (Philadelphia: Temple University Press, 1975), 83, 87.

25. Lesley Willis, "'A Sadder and a Wiser Rat / He Rose the Morrow Morn': Echoes of the Romantics in Kenneth Grahame's *The Wind in the Willows*," *Children's Literature Association Quarterly* 13, no. 3 (1988) 107–11; Richard Gillin, "Romantic Echoes in the Willows," *Children's Literature 16* (New Haven: Yale University Press, 1988), 169–74.

26. Margaret Meek, "The Limits of Delight," *Books for Keeps* 68 (May 1991), 24, 25.

4. Main Streams and Backwaters: Narrative and Structure

1. Jay Williams, "Reflections on *The Wind in the Willows.*" Signal 21 (1976), 104.

2. Humphrey Carpenter, *Secret Gardens*, 169.

3. Michael Mendolson, "*The Wind in the Willows* and the Plotting of Contrast," *Children's Literature* 16 (New Haven: Yale Unversity Press, 1988), 127–44.

4. Elspeth Grahame, *First Whispers of "The Wind in the Willows"* (London: Methuen, 1944), 2; Chalmers, *Kenneth Grahame*, 121.

5. David Gooderson, "Introduction" to Kenneth Grahame, *My Dearest Mouse: "The Wind in the Willows" Letters* (London: Pavilion/Michael Joseph, 1988), 12.

6. Grahame, *My Dearest Mouse*, 18–23.

7. Ibid., 2.

8. Lois Kuznets, "Toad's Journey to Buggleton or Kenneth Grahame's Trip from Bedside to Book," in *Proceedings of the Thirteenth Annual Conference of the Children's Literature Association*, edited by Susan R. Gannon and Ruth Anne Thompson (West Lafayette, Ind.: Children's Literature Association, 1988), 78.

9. Eleanor Grahame, "The Story of *The Wind in the Willows*: How It Came to Be Written" (1950), 2, cited by Peter Green, *Kenneth Grahame*, 266.

10. Peter Haining, *Paths to the River Bank: The Origin of* The Wind in the Willows: From the Writings of Kenneth Grahame (London: Souvenir Press, 1983), 95, 99.

11. John Moore, *Dance and Skylark* (London: Collins, 1951), 171–72.

12. Jonathan Culler, "Defining Narrative Units," in *Style and Structure in Literature*, edited by Roger Fowler (Oxford: Basil Blackwell, 1975), 138–41. See also Peter Hunt, *Criticism, Theory and Children's Literature* (Oxford: Basil Blackwell, 1991), 121–27.

13. Jerome K. Jerome, *Three Men in a Boat* [1889] (Harmondsworth, Eng.: Penguin, 1957), 136.

14. Roger Sale, *Fairy Tales and After: From Snow White to E. B. White* (Cambridge, Mass.: Harvard University Press, 1978), 185.

15. Neil Philip, "*The Wind in the Willows*: The Vitality of a Classic," in *Children and Their Books*, edited by Gillian Avery and Julia Briggs (Oxford: Clarendon Press, 1989), 307.

16. Carpenter, *Secret Gardens*, 154.

17. Michael Mendelson, "*The Wind in the Willows* and the Plotting of Contrasts", 130–31.

18. Ibid., 132.

19. Ibid., 139.

20. Sarah Gilead, "The Undoing of Idyll in *The Wind in the Willows*," *Children's Literature* 16 (New Haven: Yale University Press, 1988), 156–57.

5. Natural History: Characters, Animals, and Personal Symbolism

1. Fadiman, "Professionals and Confessionals," 281.

2. Carpenter, *Secret Gardens*, 17.

3. Arthur Ransome, "A Letter to the Editor [of *The Junior Bookshelf*]" in *Chosen for Children*, edited by Marcus Crouch and Edward Blishen (London: The Library Association, 1977), 6.

4. Robson, "On *The Wind in the Willows*", 127.

5. Quoted by Peter Haining, *Paths to the River Bank*, 12.

6. Margaret Blount, *Animal Land* (London: Hutchinson, 1974), 148.

7. Jay Williams, "Reflections on *The Wind in the Willows*," *Signal* 21 (Sept. 1976), 106.

8. A. A. Milne, *Toad of Toad Hall*, vii.

9. Naomi Lewis, "Kenneth Grahame" in *Twentieth Century Children's Writers*, edited by Tracy Chevalier, 3d ed. (Chicago: St James, 1989), 396.

10. Meek, "The Limits of Delight," 25.

11. Margery Fisher, *Classics for Children and Young People*, 37.

12. Robson, "On *The Wind in the Willows*," 119–20

13. Mary Haynes, "*The Wind in the Willows*—A Classic for Children?," 122.

14. Fred Inglis, *The Promise of Happiness: Value and Meaning in Children's Fiction* (Cambridge, Eng.: Cambridge University Press, 1981), 119.

15. Blount, *Animal Land*, 148.

16. A. A. Milne, *Toad of Toad Hall*, vii.

17. George and Weedon Grossmith, *The Diary of a Nobody* [1892] (Harmondsworth, Eng.: Penguin, 1965), 19, 83.

18. Robson, "On *The Wind in the Willows*," 127.

19. Carpenter, *Secret Gardens*, 167.

20. Inglis, *The Promise of Happiness*, 119.

21. Chalmers, *Kenneth Grahame*, 144.

22. Blount, *Animal Land*, 148; Inglis, *The Promise of Happiness*, 119.

23. Carpenter, *Secret Gardens*, 164.

24. Humphrey Carpenter and Mari Prichard, *The Oxford Companion to Children's Literature* (Oxford: Oxford University Press, 1984), 574.

25. Oscar Wilde, *The Happy Prince and Other Stories* [1888] (Harmondsworth, Eng.: Penguin, 1962), 35.

26. Meek, "The Limits of Delight," 24–25.

27. Carpenter, *Secret Gardens*, 159.

28. Lesley Willis. "A Sadder and a Wiser Rat," 109.

29. Carpenter, *Secret Gardens*, 169, 167.

30. C. S. Lewis, "On Three Ways of Writing for Children" in Sheila Egoff et al., *Only Connect*, 212–13.

31. Robson, "On *The Wind in the Willows*," 128.

32. Kuznets, *Kenneth Grahame*, 105–6.

33. Inglis, *The Promise of Happiness*, 119; Blount, *Animal Land*, 148.

34. Richard Jefferies, *Amaryllis at the Fair* [1886] (London: Dent, 1949) 204.

35. Georgina Battiscombe, "Exile from the Golden City," (*Times Literary Supplement* (13 March 1959), reprinted in *The Cool Web*, edited by Margaret Meek et al. (London: The Bodley Head, 1977), 288.

36. Nicholas Tucker, *The Child and the Book* (Cambridge: Cambridge University Press, 1981), 103.

37. Nicholas Tucker, "The Children's Falstaff," (*Times Literary Supplement* (26 June, 1969), repinted in *Suitable For Children?*, edited by Nicholas Tucker (London: Sussex University Press, 1976), 163.

38. Blount, *Animal Land*, 148; Inglis, *The Promise of Happiness*, 119; Tucker, *The Child and the Book*, 101; Robson, "On *The Wind in the Willows*," 137.

39. Sarah Gilead, "The Undoing of Idyll," 149.

40. Christopher Clausen, "Home and Away in Children's Fiction," *Children's Literature 10* (New Haven: Yale University Press, 1982), 148.

41. Carpenter, *Secret Gardens*, 164.

42. Peter Green, *Kenneth Grahame*, 260.

43. Gilead, "The Undoing of Idyll," 156.

44. Margery Fisher, *Who's Who in Children's Books* (London: Weidenfeld and Nicholson, 1975), 354.

45. Williams, "Reflections," 106.

46. Beatrix Potter, quoted in Leslie Linder, *A History of the Writings of Beatrix Potter* (London: Warne, 1971), 175.

6. Undercurrents and Whirlpools: Political and Universal Themes

1. Peter Green, *Kenneth Grahame*, 274.

2. Chalmers, *Kenneth Grahame*, 144–45.

3. Haining, *Paths to the River Bank*, 35–37.

4. Rudyard Kipling, *The Jungle Book* (Oxford: Oxford University Press, 1987), 26.

5. Robert Leeson, *Reading and Righting: The Past, Present and Future of Fiction for the Young* (London: Collins, 1985), 104.

6. Chalmers, *Kenneth Grahame*, 62.

7. Jan Needle, *Wild Wood* (London: Methuen, 1982), 106–7.

8. Haynes, "*The Wind in the Willows*—A Classic for Children?," 120.

9. Peter Green, *Kenneth Grahame*, 126.

10. Ibid., 348.

11. Arthur Ransome, *Coot Club* (London: Cape, 1934), 274.

12. Tony Watkins, "'Making a Break for the Real England,'" 34.

13. Tony Watkins, "Cultural Studies, New Historicism and Children's Literature," in *Literature for Children: Contemporary Criticism*, edited by Peter Hunt (London: Routledge, 1992), 190.

14. H. V. Morton, *In Search of England* [1927] (Harmondsworth, Eng.: Penguin, 1959), 255.

15. John Moore, *Brensham Village* [1946] (London: Pan, 1971), 93.

16. Edith Nesbit, *The Railway Children* (1906; Oxford University Press, 1991), 19.

17. Carpenter, *Secret Gardens*, 163.

7. The Wind in the Reeds—The Eddies of Style

1. Peter Green, "Introduction" to *The Wind in the Willows* (Oxford: Oxford University Press, 1983), xvi–xvii.

2. Jerome, *Three Men in a Boat*, 69, 68.

3. Ibid., 118–19.

4. Richard Jefferies, *Bevis* (1882; Oxford: Oxford University Press, 1989), 23.

5. Robson, "On *The Wind in the Willows*," 152.

6. Somerset Maugham, *Cakes and Ale* (1930), quoted by Philip, "*The Wind in the Willows*: The Vitality of a Classic," 309.

7. Philip, "*The Wind in the Willows*, The Vitality of a Classic," 309.

8. Robson, quoted by Carpenter, *Secret Gardens*, 154.

9. Quoted in E. S. Turner, *Boys Will Be Boys* (Harmondsworth, Eng.: Penguin, 1976), 45.

10. Edith Nesbit, *The Railway Children* (Oxford: Oxford University Press, 1991), 61.

11. Jan Needle, *Wild Wood*, 63 (emphasis added).

12. A. A. Milne, *Toad of Toad Hall*, 73.

13. Peter Green, *Kenneth Grahame*, 64

14. Peter Green, "Introduction" to *The Wind in the Willows*, xvii.

15. See above, chapter 3, note 25.

16. Poss. "An Epic in Arcadia: *The Wind in the Willows*," 85.

8. "A Book for Youth"

1. Barbara Wall, *The Narrator's Voice* (London: Macmillan, 1991), 142.

2. Robson, "On *The Wind in the Willows*," 143.

3. Wall, *The Narrator's Voice*, 35.

4. Ibid., 142.

5. Quoted in Peter Hunt, ed., *Children's Literature: The Development of Criticism* (London: Routledge, 1990), 51–52.

6. C. S. Lewis, "On Three Ways of Writing for Children," 211.

7. Meek, "The Limits of Delight," 25.

8. Michele Landsberg, *The World of Children's Books* (London: Simon and Schuster, 1988), 146.

9. A. A. Milne, "A Household Book," 89.

9. Approaches to Teaching

1. See Robert Whitehead, *Children's Literature: Strategies of Teaching* (Englewood Cliffs, N.J.: Prentice-Hall, 1968); Alan C. Purves and Dianne L. Monson, *Experiencing Children's Literature* (Glenview, Ill.: Scott, Foresman) 1984; Aidan Chambers: *The Reading Environment: How Adults Help Children Enjoy Books* (South Woodchester: Thimble Press, 1991); Michael Benton and Geoff Fox, *Teaching Literature, Nine to Fourteen* (Oxford: Oxford University Press, 1985).

2. See Peter Hunt, *Criticism, Theory and Children's Literature*; Peter Hunt, ed., *Children's Literature: The Development of Criticism* (London: Routledge, 1990).

3. See Edward B. Jenkinson, *Censors in the Classroom* (New York: Avon, 1982); Mark West, *Children, Culture and Controversy* (Hamden, Conn.: Archon Press, 1988); Mark West, *Trust Your Children: Voices Against Censorship in Children's Literature* (New York: Neal-Schuman, 1988).

4. Ursula K. le Guin, "This Fear of Dragons" in *The Thorny Paradise: Writers on Writing for Children*, edited by Edward Blishen (Harmondsworth, Eng.: Kestrel [Penguin], 1975) 87.

5. Aidan Chambers, "Letter from England: Great Leaping Lapins," *The Horn Book Magazine* 49, no. 3 (1973), 255.

Bibliography

Primary Sources

Dream Days. With illustrations and decorations by Ernest H. Shepard. London: John Lane, The Bodley Head, 1930. First published in 1898.

My Dearest Mouse—The Wind in the Willows *Letters.* Edited by David Gooderson. London: Pavilion, 1988.

Pagan Papers. London: Elkin Matthews and John Lane, 1893.

The Golden Age. London: John Lane, 1895. Illustrated by Lois Lenski, London: John Lane, The Bodley Head/New York: The John Lane Company, 1921.

The Wind in the Willows. London: Methuen, 1908. New York, Macmillan, 1989. [1st edition with frontispiece by Graham Robinson. Illustrated editions: Paul Branson (1913), Nancy Barnhart (1922), Wyndham Payne (1927), E. H. Shepard (1931), Arthur Rackham (1940), Roberta Carter Clark (1966), Michael Hague (1980), John Burningham (1983), Harry Hargreaves (1983).]

Milne, A. A. *Toad of Toad Hall: A Play from Kenneth Grahame's Book* The Wind in the Willows. London: Methuen, 1929. London: Methuen (Modern Classics), 1940.

Needle, Jan. *Wild Wood.* London: Andre Deutsch, 1981. London: Methuen (Magnet Books), 1982.

Secondary Sources

Books

Chalmers, Patrick. *Kenneth Graham: Life, Letters, and Unpublished Work.* London: Methuen, 1933.

Graham, Eleanor. *Kenneth Grahame.* London: The Bodley Head, 1963.

Grahame, Elspeth, ed., *First Whisper of* The Wind in the Willows, *by Kenneth Grahame.* London: Methuen, 1944; Philadelphia: Lippincot, 1944.

Green, Peter. *Beyond the Wild Wood: The World of Kenneth Grahame, Author of* The Wind in the Willows. Exeter: Webb and Bower, 1982; New York: Facts on File, 1983.

————. Kenneth Grahame, *1859–1932: A Study of His Life and Works, and Times.* London: John Murray, 1959. [Cleveland World Publishing, 1969.]

Haining. Peter. *Paths to the River Bank: The Origins of The Wind in the Willows* from the Writings of Kenneth Grahame. London: Souvenir Press, 1983.

Kuznets, Lois R. *Kenneth Grahame.* Boston: Twayne, 1987.

General Studies Containing Discussion of The Wind in the Willows

Blount, Margaret. *Animal Land. The Creatures of Children's Fiction.* London: Hutchinson, 1974.

Carpenter, Humphrey. *Secret Gardens: A Study of the Golden Age of Children's Literature.* London: Allen and Unwin, 1985; Unwin Hyman (1987); Boston: Houghton Mifflin, 1985.

————, and Mari Prichard. *The Oxford Companion to Children's Literature.* Oxford: Oxford University Press, 1984.

Fisher, Margery. *Classics for Children and Young People.* South Woodchester, Eng.: Thimble Press, 1986.

Green, Roger Lancelyn. *Tellers of Tales: Children's Books and Their Authors from 1800 to 1968.* 4th ed. London: Ward, 1965.

Inglis, Fred. *The Promise of Happiness: Value and Meaning in Children's Fiction.* Cambridge, Eng.: Cambridge University Press, 1981.

Sale, Roger. *Fairy Tales and After: From Snow White to E. B. White.* Cambridge, Mass.: Harvard University Press, 1978.

Townsend, John Rowe. *Written for Children: An Outline for English Language Children's Literature.* 2nd rev. ed. Harmondsworth, Eng.: Penguin, 1983.

Bibliography

Wall, Barbara. *The Narrator's Voice: The Dilemma of Children's Fiction.* London: Macmillan. 1991.

Articles

Battiscombe, Georgina. "Exile from the Golden City." In *The Cool Web: The Pattern of Children's Reading,* edited by Margaret Meek, Aidan Warlow, and Griselda Barton, 284–90. London: The Bodley Head, 1977.

Clausen, Christopher. "Home and Away in Children's Fiction." *Children's Literature* 10 (1982): 141–52.

Cripps, Elizabeth. "Kenneth Grahame: Children's Author?" *Children's Literature in Education* 13 (1981): 15–23.

Fadiman, Clifton. "Professionals and Confessionals: Dr. Seuss and Kenneth Grahame." In *Only Connect: Readings on Children's Literature,* edited by Sheila Egoff, G. T. Stubbs, and L. F. Ashley, 276–83. Toronto: Oxford University Press, 2nd ed. 1980.

Gilead, Sarah. "The Undoing Idyll in *The Wind in the Willows.*" *Children's Literature* 16 (1988): 145–58.

Gillin, Richard. "Romantic Echoes in the Willows." *Children's Literature* 16 (1988): 169–74.

Green, Peter. "Introduction" to Kenneth Grahame, *The Wind in the Willows.* Oxford: Oxford University Press, 1983.

———. "The Rentier's Rural Dream." *Times Literary Supplement* (26 November 1982): 1299–1301.

Green, Roger Lancelyn. "Reed Talk: The Genius of Kenneth Graham." *The Scots Magazine* (July 1945): 262–67.

Haynes Mary. "*The Wind in the Willows*: A Classic for Children?" *International Review of Children's Literature and Librarianship* 4, no. 2 (1989): 115-29.

Hunt, Peter. "Dialogue and Dialectic: Language and Class in *The Wind in the Willows.*" *Children's Literature* 16 (1988): 159–68.

———. "Necessary Misreadings: Directions in Narrative Theory for Children's Literature." *Studies in the Literary Imagination* 18 (1985): 107–21. Revised version in his *Criticism, Theory and Children's Literature.* Oxford: Blackwell, 1991.

Kuznets, Lois. "Kenneth Grahame and Father Nature, or Whither Blows *The Wind in the Willows?*" *Children's Literature* 16 (1988): 175–81.

———. "Toad Hall Revisited." *Children's Literature* 7 (1977): 115–28.

Lippmann, Carlee, "All the Comforts of Home." *Antioch Review* 41 (1983): 409–40.

McGillis, Roderick. "Utopian Hopes: Criticism Beyond Itself?" *Children's Association Quarterly* 9, no. 4 (1984–85): 184–86.

Macy, G. "Arthur Rackham and *The Wind in the Willows.*" *Horn Book* 16, no. 3 (1940): 152–58.

Meek. Margaret. "Blind Spot: The Limits of Delight." *Books for Keeps* 68 (1991): 24–25.

Mendelsohn, Michael. "*The Wind in the Willows* and the Plotting of Contrast." *Children's Literature* 16 (1988): 127–44.

Milne, A. A. "A Household Book" in his *Not That It Matters*. London: Methuen, 1919.

Philip, Neil. "Kenneth Grahame's *The Wind in the Willows*: A Companionable Vitality." In *Touchstones: Reflections on the Best in Children's Literature*, vol. 1. West Lafayette, Ind.: Children's Literature Association, 1985

Pocock, Guy. "*The Wind in the Willows.*" *The Schoolmistress* (6 September 1934): 579.

Poss, Geraldine D. "An Epic in Arcadia, the Pastoral World of *The Wind in the Willows.*" *Children's Literature* 4 (1975): 80–90.

Robson, W. W. "On *The Wind in the Willows.*" In his *The Definition of Literature and Other Essays*. Cambridge, Eng.: 1982.

Scheider, Richard L. "*The Wind in the Willows*: Lyric Prose into Music." *Literature in Performance* 2 (1982): 64–68.

Shepard, E. H. "Illustrating *The Wind in the Willows.*" *Horn Book* 30 (April 1954): 83–86.

Sterck, Kenneth. "Rereading *The Wind in the Willows.*" *Children's Literature in Education* 12 (1973).

Steig, Michael. "At the Back of *The Wind in the Willows*: An Experiment in Biographical and Autobiographical Interpretation." *Victorian Studies* 24 (1981): 303–23.

Tucker, Nicholas. "The Children's Falstaff." In *Suitable for Children? Controversies in Children's Literature*, edited by Nicholas Tucker. London: Sussex University Press, 1976, 160–64.

Waddey, Lucy. "Home in Children's Fiction, Three Patterns." *Children's Literature Association Quarterly* 8 (1983): 13–14.

Watkins, Tony. "Making a Break for the Real England: The River-Bankers Revisited." *Children's Literature Association Quarterly* 9, no. 1 (1984): 34–35.

———. "Cultural Studies, New Historicism and Children's Literature." In *Literature for Children: Contemporary Criticism*, edited by Peter Hunt. London: Routledge, 1992, 173–95.

Bibliography

Williams, Jay. "Reflections on *The Wind in the Willows*." *Signal* 21 (1976): 103–7.

Willis, Lesley. " 'A Sadder and a Wiser Rat/He Rose the Morrow Morn': Echoes of the Romantics in Kenneth Grahame's *The Wind in the Willows*." *Children's Literature Association Quarterly* 13, no. 3 (1988): 107–11.

Zanger, Julius. "Goblins, Worlocks and Weasels: Classic Fantasy and the Industrial Revolution." *Children's Literature in Education* 8, no. 4 (1977): 154–62.

Index

About the Author

Peter Hunt teaches English and Children's Literature at the University of Wales, Cardiff, UK. He was written widely on criticism and children's literature, and his books include *Criticism, Theory, and Children's Literature* (1991), *Approaching Arthur Ransome* (1992), and *An Introduction to Children's Literature* (1994). He has edited two collections of essays, *Children's Literature: The Development of Criticism* (1990) and *Literature for Children: Contemporary Criticism* (1992), and Richard Jefferies' *Bevis*. Among his six books for children and young adults are *Backtrack* (1986) and *Going Up* (1989). He has lectured at more than fifty universities worldwide, and has held visiting academic posts at the University of Michigan, Massachusetts Institute of Technology, and San Diego State University, and at the University of Wollongong, Australia.

Peter Hunt lives in the Cotswold Hills in Gloucestershire, England, with his wife Sarah, and four daughters, Felicity, Amy, Abigail, and Chloë.